BACK ROADS of California

School at Knight's Ferry

Sunset

BACK ROADS
of California

Sketches and Trip Notes by EARL THOLLANDER

Supervising Editor: JACK McDOWELL

Special Travel Features: *Dorothy Krell*
Design Consultant: *John Channing Rudd*
Layout and Travel Research: *Carol Goforth*

LANE PUBLISHING CO. • MENLO PARK, CALIFORNIA

ENJOY THE ROADS!
DON'T RUIN THEM FOR OTHERS.

DON'T LITTER. DON'T TRESPASS
ON POSTED PROPERTY. DON'T
DAMAGE FENCES OR LEAVE GATES
OPEN. DON'T PICK CROPS
...
DRIVE CAREFULLY!

Fifth printing August 1984
Second Edition. Copyright © 1977, 1971, by Lane
Publishing Co. • Menlo Park, CA 94025.
World rights reserved. No part of this publication
may be reproduced by any mechanical,
photographic, or electronic process, or in the form
of a phonographic recording, nor may it be stored
in a retrieval system, transmitted, or otherwise
copied for public or private use without
prior written permission from the publisher.
Library of Congress No. 76-40552. ISBN
0-376-05014-4. Lithographed in the United States.

Editor, Sunset Books: David E. Clark

Front Cover: *View from Franz Valley Road, north of
Santa Rosa.* Back Cover: *Honey Run
covered bridge, east of Chico.*

ANOTHER WAY TO GET THERE

Freeways, highways, and parkways weave a busy fretwork of travel corridors over the face of California. A straight-line course is the thing today; but the shortest distance between two points is not always the most pleasurable way. Roundabout, alternate roads in the West have for several years been reported on by *Sunset Magazine,* and this book is an outgrowth of that reporting. It is a careful sampling of some of California's most interesting back roads and leisurely side trips.

A good many of those trips are over nicely paved thoroughfares paralleling main highways. Others take off on unimproved, tortuous routes whose charm is in their ruggedness. Most back-road adventurers derive great pleasure in exploring such little-known places and they delight even in occasionally getting lost. For more complete maps than are available in this book, travelers are advised to avail themselves of detailed automobile club maps (though the latter are usually available only to club members). County and local maps may be purchased in many book stores, local news-stands, or are sometimes obtainable through chambers of commerce. Always inquire locally before venturing onto remote roads, because conditions can change from one day to the next.

Earl Thollander's personal approach to travel, to art, and to writing speaks of a relaxed outlook and a love for the smallest detail, both of which qualify him as a good spokesman for ventures off the beaten track.

Because California has such a wealth of country byways, many reader favorites may not appear in this selection. Travelers are encouraged to let us know of any other good back roads they would like to share.

THE SUNSET EDITORS

Cannon Mailbox,
Mines Road near
Livermore

CONTENTS

Central Valley and the Sierra

Northern California

Tractor near Forbestown,
east of Chico

East from San Diego—San Gabriels, San Bernardinos—Bakersfield South

THE SOUTHWEST CORNER

The back roads of Southern California's western corner generally lead inland —into coastal valleys and into mountain ranges that begin in low hills near the sea and rise to timbered high country and rugged wilderness before dropping down to desert on the eastern side.

From the border to San Juan Capistrano, Interstate 5 gives access to the coastal communities at the southern end of the state, and U.S. 101 explores the shore northwest of Los Angeles. Where these travel corridors swing inland at Los Angeles, State 1 and Interstate 405 skirt the western edge of the city, never far from the ocean.

In San Diego's back country, quiet byways lead to old gold mining towns and charming mission chapels that welcome today's visitors as they welcomed the Indians whom they first served. California's history began in this southwestern corner of the state when Juan Rodriguez Cabrillo landed at Point Loma in 1542, and it was on San Diego's Presidio Hill that the first of California's twenty-one Franciscan missions was established.

Local roads meander along the cool, forested backbone of the San Jacinto Mountains that separate the wheat and orchard country of the San Jacinto Valley from the desert of the Coachella Valley and the sun-drenched resorts of the Palm Springs area. Through the San Bernardino Mountains, highest of the ranges that separate Los Angeles from the inland desert, winds Rim of the World Drive. It leads to resort areas around Lake Arrowhead and Big Bear Lake, and from it quiet side roads take off into wooded hills and valleys. Stretching from near the coast to the Mojave Desert, the San Gabriel Mountains form the northern skyline of Los Angeles. Spur roads from foothill communities penetrate their front-range canyons, and the Angeles Crest Highway gives access to higher country and views into the wild and rough San Gabriel Wilderness Area.

The Lonely Route from Chula Vista to Descanso

At Chula Vista, turn off Interstate Highway 5 onto County Road S17. It is also called E Street and later becomes Bonita Road. Where Bonita goes left, keep right on San Miguel Road to Proctor Valley Road. At Jamul go south 1.2 miles and turn right to visit Saint Mary Church.

I drove up the steep, rutty, dirt road past Indian dwellings, finally parking and walking the last section of road.

SAINT MARY CHURCH,
THE INDIAN CHURCH AT JAMUL

"This is St. Mary church", a large Indian lady told me ··· "It is only used for funerals." The adjoining cemetery is colorful, for each cross is festooned with plastic flowers and paper streamers. The crosses are mostly wooden and painted, either black or white. Somehow, the plastic flowers were used so creatively and lovingly I didn't mind their fakery.

Out of Jamul I traveled on Lyons and Japatul Valley Roads to Descanso and Interstate 8. The trip from Chula Vista had been 37 miles.

LYONS PEAK AND FIRE LOOKOUT FROM LYONS VALLEY ROAD

San Bernardino South, the Leisurely Way

San Bernardino to "Rim of the World Drive" via Highways 18 or 30 is about 20 uphill miles.

Past Arrowbear Lake you can turn off toward Green Valley Lake, but before reaching there drive left onto a dirt road heading for Big Pine Flats and Holcomb Valley. I enjoyed the day going through this historic gold mining country. I think I started at the right place, too, because other roads in are straight and easy. I built up considerable respect for the land, winding through forests of white fir, cedar, piñon pine, ponderosa, and jeffrey.

BELLEVILLE'S LAST SHACK

HITCHCOCK RANCH
IN HOLCOMB VALLEY

Farther on, I inspected the area where the town of Belleville once stood. I sketched the only dwelling visible, sitting picturesquely among the rocks. I located it from "Hangman's Tree."

A marker here says "Holcomb Valley, named for William Francis "Bill" Holcomb, pioneer prospector who, in this valley discovered southern California's richest gold field, May 5, 1860."

I traveled from Holcomb Valley on Highways 18 and 38 past the San Gorgonio Wilderness.

TAHQUITZ PEAK,
SAN JACINTO MOUNTAINS

HEADSTONE AT PALA

The Little-Known Chapel at Pala

The only remaining asistencia, or sub-mission, of a score or more that were established by the California missions is San Antonio de Pala. It is a branch of Mission San Luis Rey, which lies five miles east of Oceanside. Still in active use as a parish church, Pala serves the Pauma Indians as it did when it was founded in 1815. At its peak, the chapel was used by more than a thousand Indians, who worked the fields in the sheltered San Luis Rey River valley. After secularization of the missions by the Mexican government and the American occupation that followed, the church property passed into private ownership. San Antonio de Pala was closed until 1903 when the Landmarks Club purchased it and returned it to the Catholic Church.

THE CAMPANILE, SAN ANTONIO DE PALA

Heading to Banning, I turned south
and went west through the San Jacinto
Mountains toward Mountain Center,
then went west to Hemet on State 74.
Through Diamond Valley, south of Hemet,
I came to the village of Sage and its
old fashioned gas station.
Pala Road turns off Highway 71 farther south
and leads to Mission San Antonio de Pala.
School was out for the day and I was all but
surrounded by Indian boys and girls watching me
draw. Even the principal of the school gave
an approving smile as she passed me in the garden.
In 1916 a flood destroyed the campanile
It was immediately restored, using the same
materials. A young Indian boy told me that
he had been allowed to ring the campanile bells
once for mass. They are also rung, he said,
when someone dies and during the funeral procession.

The Old Ridge Road
from Saugus to Gorman

Interstate 5, near Saugus, took me to
Castaic and the Lake Hughes Road.
Instead of continuing on the Lake
Road I turned left onto the
Old Ridge Road.

Concrete and steel rods hold the
historic road in place. The aged
surface is still in evidence.
It is worthwhile traveling this
road to see views of huge
uninhabited mountain masses.
Look toward the setting sun, and
the mountains are hazy and blue.
Look east, and they are pink.

THE OLD RIDGE ROAD

THE OLD
RIDGE ROAD

A 28-mile journey the Ridge
Road connects with county road
N2 and Highway 138.

San Gabriel Mountain Link—
Interstate 5 to Interstate 15

Highway 138 heads east from
Interstate 5 near Gorman and Lebec.
County Road N2 (Pine Canyon Road) branches
off 138 to the right 9 miles later.

APPLE VANED BARN,
PINE CANYON ROAD

SOME SOUTHERN
CALIFORNIA
WILDFLOWERS

TREE TOBACCO IN BLOOM
WITH ITS BRIGHT YELLOW,
TRUMPET-LIKE FLOWERS

BLACK SAGE GIVES A
PURPLE HUE TO A
WHOLE MOUNTAINSIDE

Wildflowers and Wild Waters: Three Canyon Drives

Three gentle canyons near the west end of the San Gabriel Mountains can be used as approaches to the poppy fields of Antelope Valley to the north, and connecting roads near and above the heads of the canyons make for convenient loop trips from Interstate 5. Picnic spots are many and inviting along the way.

Bouquet Canyon, with its weekend cabins and roadside campgrounds, is the most popular. Elizabeth Lake Canyon, least altered of the three, is perhaps the prettiest. Near the head of Bouquet Canyon, the road swings around Bouquet Reservoir, part of the Los Angeles Aqueduct, built at a cost of twenty-three million dollars to supply water to the San Fernando Valley. The drive over to Green Valley and the head of San Francisquito Canyon goes through the site of St. Francis Dam, which broke without warning on March 13, 1928, shortly after it was completed, sending billions of gallons of water rushing down San Francisquito Creek, destroying bridges, homes, crops, and killing some five hundred people.

You can go to Three Points, then onto Elizabeth Lake Road along the San Andreas Earthquake Fault. Other roads to explore are Elizabeth Canyon Road, Green Valley, San Francisquito Canyon and Bouquet Canyon roads.

STORE AND SALOON, 1909
THREE POINTS

THE JOSTLED ROCKS OF DEVIL'S PUNCHBOWL

Devil's Punchbowl and the Rock Candy Mountains

In the semidesert country on the north slopes of the San Gabriel Mountains, a 25-mile-long displacement of a spectacular rock formation crossed by the San Andreas Fault resulted in two upthrusts known as Devil's Punchbowl and the Rock Candy Mountains. Devil's Punchbowl is now a Los Angeles County park. A paved road leads to a canyon rim overlooking the formations, and a mile-long trail down into the main canyon gives a close-up look at dun-colored, weather-etched rocks and cliffs.

The Punchbowl is actually three bowls, carved by streams flowing toward the desert. Exposed fins of the jutting outcrop extend for three miles in a band that reaches a width of nearly a mile and stands out sharply against the surrounding chaparral.

The Rock Candy Mountains, the other part of the original formation, can be seen for about a half mile on both sides of State 138 near Cajon Junction, southeast of Punchbowl.

On Table Mountain
trees are shaped
by winter storms.
I sketched with
a swift, cold wind
making me grip my
drawing board tightly
to keep it from flying.
Out of the mountains past
Wrightwood I reached
Highway 138 and then
Interstate 15. The trip
had been 120 miles.

BIG PINE ON TABLE MOUNTAIN

Santa Barbara — Santa Ynez Valley — Santa Maria

It is 30 miles from Santa Barbara to Santa Ynez over San Marcos Pass. Foxen Canyon Road after Los Olivos goes to Sisquoc and Santa Maria.

Near Solvang there is pleasing country landscape on Armour, Happy Canyon, Roblar, and Alamo Pintado roads. At Ballard schoolhouse on Base Line Avenue, where I stopped to sketch, the Mother's Club of the 1883 red and white school were having their annual, fund-raising chicken barbecue. A little girl asked me, "Did you draw all that?" Another, annoyed that a contemporary would ask such an obvious question, replied, "What do you think he did, tear it out of a magazine?"

I said to a small boy just arriving breathlessly on the scene, "What a nice place to have a picnic." He replied, "What a great place to YELL!" One little girl saw someone photographing the historic school and said to me, quite casually, "but your drawing will be nicer and quite special." I'd never felt more highly complimented.

BALLARD SCHOOLHOUSE

HIGH ON THE HILL,
SISQUOC CHURCH, 1875

It is not far from Ballard to Mission Santa Inés and the Danish town of Solvang. Atterdag Road, off Highway 246, becomes Chalk Hill Road (Ballard Canyon Road) out of Solvang, and along here is the neatly kept Danish Cemetery. Many of the graves are simple wooden crosses, with names freshly re painted. Chalk Hill brings you to Foxen Canyon Road, Highway 166, and Santa Maria. I stopped to sketch Sisquoc Church along Foxen Canyon. The eaves are riddled with woodpecker holes. From a larger hole a mean-looking hawk, too young to fly, screamed for food.

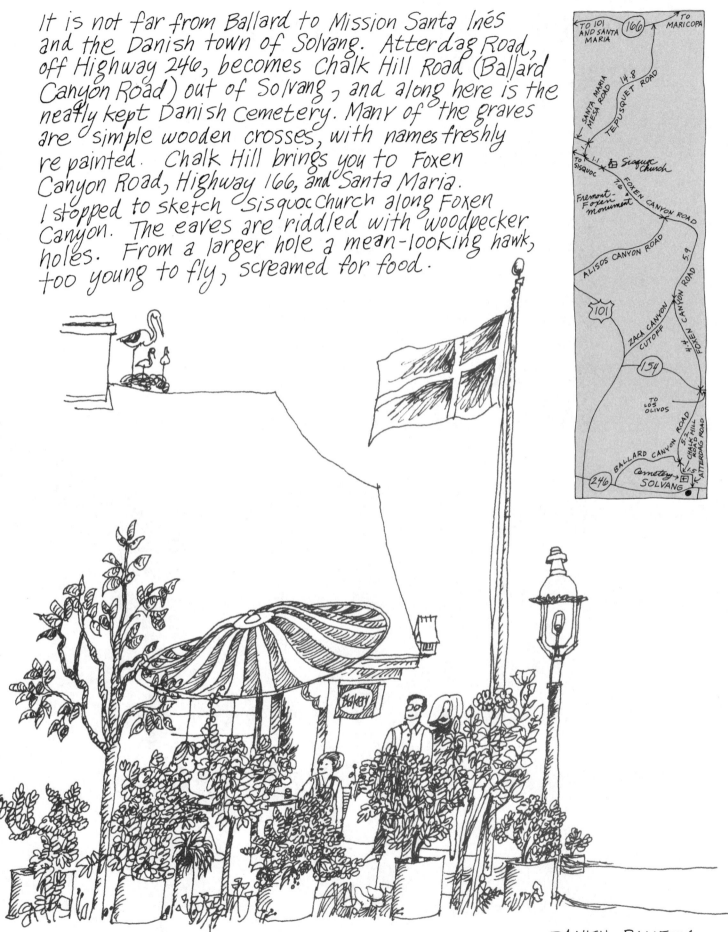

DANISH BAKERY, SOLVANG

From Bakersfield to Ventura, through Los Padres National Forest

About 43 miles south of Bakersfield is Frazier Mountain Road through Los Padres National Forest.

Clearing Frazier Park and Lake of the Woods, you can enjoy a 30-mile, leisurely drive through Los Padres National Forest. It is piñon pine country with an occasional "grandaddy" pine towering over the diminutive piñons. I eventually reached Highway 33-39 miles from Ojai. Back roads of Ojai are lined by orange groves and thick rock walls. Most attractive was Carne Road with its date palms and flowers.

MOUNTAIN RIDGE,
LOS PADRES NATIONAL FOREST

OJAI'S ORANGES
AND SMUDGE POTS

Historical Fort Tejon

Valley oaks shade the restored buildings of Fort Tejon, a cool oasis along Interstate 5 north of Tejon Pass. The fort was established in 1854. It originally was headquarters for the 1st U.S. Dragoons, sent to protect the friendly Indians of the Sebastian Reservation and to control Grapevine Pass, through which rustlers drove cattle and horses from the San Joaquin Valley to southern markets. Later it housed units of the U.S. Army Camel Corps, which experimented with the use of camels for transporting supplies to isolated posts in the southwest deserts—an idea that was abandoned when it was found that the tender feet of the camels were not suited to the rocky soil of the Fort Tejon region. Ten years after its founding, the fort became inactive. Today the 210-acre property is a historical monument. The visitors' center contains displays of artifacts relating to the fort, and oak-shaded tables make inviting spots to spread a picnic lunch.

Anza-Borrego, Mojave Byways — Saline,
Panamint, and Tehachapi Valleys

THE SOUTHERN DESERT

The lure of the desert lies away from the main routes, in the lonely expanses that stretch to a purple-shadowed mountain horizon. Here, Joshua trees replace billboards along the roadside. Desert creatures scurry across rocks, and windswept dunes register the quiet comings and goings of wildlife.

Just above the Mexican border, Interstate 80 heads east from San Diego to Yuma and beyond. It provides access to roads leading into Anza-Borrego Desert State Park and to the developments around the Salton Sea. Farther north, Interstate 10 reaches the Palm Springs resorts and Joshua Tree National Monument. Interstate 15 follows a northeasterly route through the lonely Mojave, carrying travelers between the metropolitan centers west of Los Angeles and the glitter of Las Vegas. U.S. 395 skirts the Mojave's western edge, and is joined by roads that reach into the stillness of the Panamint and Saline valleys and the strange landscape of Death Valley National Monument.

Adventuresome travelers can explore narrow, fantastically eroded canyons and drive winding roads that climb to far-reaching vistas. They can follow routes traveled by stagecoaches in the 1850's, and peer into the dark depths of now-quiet mines and weathered buildings of old mining towns.

Following winter rains, the desert comes alive with a brief but spectacular display of wildflowers. Thorny ocotillo stalks become tipped with heavy clusters of red flowers; pink verbena blankets the dunes; California poppies streak the hillsides with brilliant orange; yuccas send up huge, creamy plumes.

The casual back road traveler should exercise extreme caution in exploring unmarked desert trails that branch invitingly off the main highway. Many such roads begin on level, firm ground, then dip into gullies that form sand traps. During the rainy season such washes become dangerous raging torrents from water runoff. Unpaved desert roads should never be explored without advice from local residents.

Along the Butterfield Stage Route

The Overland Stage Route (County Road S2) more or less follows the old Butterfield Stage Coach Route. You can begin at Ocotillo, along Interstate 8.

Bow Willow in Anza-Borrego Desert State Park is a good campground. Farther north is a side road to Mountain Palm Springs. You can drive within one-half mile of the palms, then hike to the little oasis. The sandy ground I walked on glittered with mica. The palms give refuge to the birds, and they sang continuously as I sketched.

THE OASIS AT MOUNTAIN PALM SPRINGS, ANZA-BORREGO DESERT

TRAVELING THE BUTTERFIELD
STAGECOACH ROAD,
VALLECITO CREEK

One and a half miles beyond Mountain Palm Springs is a road marked "GREAT SOUTHERN OVERLAND STAGE ROUTE OF 1849" and "RANGER STATION 1.4 MILES".
Go 4 miles along this road and you intersect the Vallecito Creekbed. Turn left and follow the creekbed back to the highway and you will have traveled over the original Butterfield Stage Route. The creekbed is sandy, and it is not an official road, so check with the Ranger next to Martin's Trailer Park on this trip. There were no stagecoach tracks, but a feeling of history was with me on this 9½-mile ride. At Vallecito County Park, farther along County Road S2, is the re-created stage station, completed in 1934. In Box Canyon you can see the tracks worn into the rocks by many a stagecoach. Box Canyon is about 8 miles beyond Vallecito.

VALLECITO STAGE STATION

The old Butterfield Stage Route
goes up San Felipe Canyon
connecting with Highway 79, with
4 miles to go to Warner Springs.
At Oak Grove, thirteen miles
beyond, the old stage station
still stands. The adobe facade
has been covered. "People
stuck their fingers in the old
wall and said, ooh!, it really
is adobe," the owner told me.
He put wooden siding up to
keep the building from dissolving.

WARREN T. HALL RESIDENCE,
BUTTERFIELD STAGE
STATION MANAGER, 1858,
OAK GROVE

TELESCOPE AT
MOUNT PALOMAR

The World's Largest Telescope

From the great silver dome of the observatory on Mount Palomar, the world's largest reflector telescope photographs stars billions of miles away. The Hale, named for astronomer George Ellery Hale, is a 200-inch telescope weighing 500 tons. It is viewed from a gallery in a dome kept at nighttime temperatures, since only a few degrees of variation can cause distortions. The observatory was completed in 1948, twenty years after the Rockefeller Foundation granted six million dollars for the project.

A diversion can be made from the Butterfield Stage Route, south of Warner Springs along Highway 79, to see three Indian Missions. The first is Santa Ysabel, on 79, 2 miles north of the town of the same name. Take Mesa Grande Road a short ½ mile north of the mission, and enjoy the country drive 8 miles to St. Dominick's Chapel. Keep going, winding down the mountain, finally, to turn left onto Highway 76. Two and one-half miles beyond Pauma Valley town, take Pauma Reservation Road one mile to see Pauma Indian Mission. I leaned against an ancient pepper tree to sketch the mission's modest campanile.

A mile south of Pauma Road, the Nate Harrison Grade will take you to Mt. Palomar. Or, for a much less rugged route, go 8 miles more along 76, then make the ascent. Seeing the telescope and the magnificent exhibit of photographs in the museum is important. I left with a greater respect and concern for our earth and for the great spaces beyond.

PAUMA INDIAN MISSION CAMPANILE

Having forsaken the
Butterfield Stage Route
for the freeways to
the west, I found
a pleasant back road
in Orange County.
Nine miles north of
San Juan Capistrano, on
Interstate 5, I turned off
at El Toro, taking Modjeska
Road and Santiago Canyon
Road to get to Tucker
Wildlife Sanctuary.
You may sit quietly there,
watching wild birds
at close range.

TUCKER
WILDLIFE
SANCTUARY

Back Road through Anza-Borrego

The most impressive drive into the desert of Anza-Borrego is to turn off Highway 79 at San Felipe Road. 4½-miles later stay on Montezuma Valley Road, County Road S22, to Borrego Springs.

The view into the desert is deep and truly astounding. Camp at Borrego-Palm Canyon Campground, for there is a delightful and instructive walk through the canyon. I drove the sandy road into Coyote Canyon next day to see the ocotillo and torch cactus in bloom and to be alone in the desert.

DRIVING IN COYOTE CANYON

OCOTILLO
ALONG COYOTE
CANYON ROAD

MOUNTAINS OF THE ANZA-BORREGO

Painted Canyon and the Salton Sea

Below Joshua Tree National Monument
Highway 195 leads to Mecca and
south to Highway 86 and the
Salton Sea. This was my lonesome
route to Anza-Borrego Desert.

Signs along the way said,
"FLASH FLOODS, WATCH FOR DEBRIS."
At one point the cliffs on either
side looked like the Grand
Canyon in miniature.

PAINTED CANYON,
EAST OF MECCA

Date palm orchards, vegetable farms, and vineyards surround Mecca, a region of vast farming projects. Going farther south on Highway 86 you pass placid Salton Sea. At Salton City the Borrego-Salton Seaway begins, heading toward the great Anza-Borrego Desert. If it is toward sundown the Santa Rosa mountains, on your right, will turn from pink to purple in the setting sun.

DATE PALMS NEAR MECCA

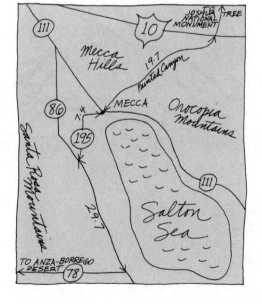

South from U.S. 40 along the Road of the Joshua Trees

Near Amboy Crater, on the Old National Trail Highway, Amboy Road goes south to Twentynine Palms. The long way through Joshua Tree National Monument, which I chose, begins at Joshua Tree, 15 miles west of here along Highway 62.

I was happy to leave the desert developments and real estate signs for the magnificence of the Joshua Tree Monument.

SHEEPHOLE MOUNTAINS, AMBOY ROAD

DESERT DWELLERS NEAR
TWENTY-NINE PALMS

JOSHUA TREE
NATIONAL MONUMENT

The rock formations are as startling as the forests of Joshua trees. Artistic rock compositions are everywhere. Mojave yucca is blooming, a huge flower head of waxy, pale yellow flowers. The nature walk at Cap Rock, along Pinto Basin Road, furnished me with a look at a delightful little creature, a desert cottontail with big eyes and white powderpuff of a tail.

ROCKS AND
JOSHUA TREES

CAP ROCK

SPLIT ROCK

Desert Ecology: The Plants Tell a Story

The meaning of high desert and low desert is illustrated in few places as vividly as in Joshua Tree National Monument. The monument is situated on a high plateau that edges a precipitous drop-off to a below-sea-level desert sink, the Coachella Valley and Salton Sea. Altitudes in the monument range from 1,000 to nearly 6,000 feet. Here, visitors may experience two Southern California deserts: low Colorado and high Mojave.

Indicator plant of the low desert, up to about 3,000 feet, is the creosote bush, but the low desert also displays such beauties as the green-trunked palo verde, the gray smoke tree, and the ocotillo and cholla cacti. The cholla is transitional and crosses over into high-desert, which is marked first by Mojave yucca and juniper. At the upper end of the yucca range is the chief indicator of the Mojave Desert, the Joshua tree. It in turn penetrates the lower edge of piñon-juniper-scrub oak woodland at about 4,200 feet, which ranges on up to the highest elevations of the monument.

Mitchell Caverns Byway off U.S. 40

Fifty miles east of Ludlow at Essex Road the 16-mile trip up to Mitchell Caverns begins.

At this elevation the beauty of the desert in spring is astounding. It is a vast garden of blooming cactus and desert plants of infinite variety. The caverns are at 4,500 feet, and the chocolate-colored mountains behind rise to 6,970 feet, with snow patches up top. Bird calls echo in the canyons. From the entrance of the caverns the view is broad.....300 square miles of the Clipper and Fenner Valleys lie below, and the Hualapai Mountains are clearly seen 85 miles from this point.

THE ROAD TO MITCHELL CAVERNS

KELSO

MITCHELL CAVERNS

BLACK CANYON RD.

Providence Mountains

KELBAKER ROAD

ESSEX ROAD 16.2

Clipper Valley

Fenner Valley

40

TO BARSTOW

Clipper Mountains

TO NEEDLES

6.4

ESSEX

OLD NATIONAL TRAIL HIGHWAY

PENSTEMON, OF THE HAIRY, YELLOW "BEARD TONGUE"

EVENING PRIMROSE, MOJAVE DESERT

Easy Spelunking in the Mojave

The only limestone caves in Southern California that are developed for visitors are perched high on the slopes of the craggy Providence Mountains in the eastern Mojave Desert, at Mitchell Caverns State Reserve. For centuries they provided shelter for nomadic Indians that roamed the desert, and later they were known to early settlers and prospectors. Around 1930, a prospector by the name of Jack Mitchell acquired the caves with a mining claim. He took up residence and opened them to the public. Then in 1956 he sold the property to the Department of Parks and Recreation.

This beautiful world of sculptured limestone was originally formed by underground water that dissolved portions of the primeval limestone. Later the water table lowered, emptying the rooms. Mineral-laden surface water dripped from the ceilings of the caverns, and, by depositing calcium carbonate, gradually created the unusually delicate stalactites, stalagmites, cave coral, and stone curtains that decorate the rooms today.

MITCHELL
CAVERNS,
MOJAVE DESERT

Possum Trot and Calico

Seven miles east of Barstow on Interstate 15, the 3-mile road to Calico begins. Possum Trot is halfway to Calico.

The late Calvin Black, mayor of Possum Trot, named the place, and he and Ruby Black were the entire population. Calvin was a doll-maker, ventriloquist, preacher, entertainer and artist. His dolls are almost life-size, and some could pedal bicycles, dance, ring bells and speak, when Calvin was alive to keep everything working.

With Ruby Black now gone, the future of Possum Trot is uncertain.

POSSUM TROT DOLL BY CALVIN BLACK

THE TRAIN AT CALICO

There's a ride to take on the
Calico and Odessa Railroad.
I sketched, then relaxed while
the train tooted and clanged
along on its 8-minute journey,
returning to pose for me
from time to time.

Toward the Tehachapi Valley

WOODFORD (KEENE POST OFFICE)
TEHACHAPI LOOP
WOODFORD-TEHACHAPI
TEHACHAPI
58
MOJAVE
58
SILVER QUEEN ROAD
MOJAVE-TROPICO RD
SOLEDAD MOUNTAIN
14
TROPICO MINE
ROSAMOND BOULEVARD
ROSAMOND

Turn off Highway 58 at Woodford (Keene Post Office) to see the Tehachapi Loop. Just south of the city of Mojave, Silver Queen Road goes past the much-mined Soledad Mountain and to the Tropico Mine.

TURN OF THE CENTURY
POST OFFICE

KEENE
POST OFFICE

From Keene to Tehachapi an old
two-lane highway passes a vantage
point where you can look down on
the "Loop". If you are lucky, or
can wait for the next freight, you
will see a train make the
historic "Loop".
The road then dips down into
the broad Tehachapi Valley and
through fields of dwarf lupine
and the green grass of springtime.
Turn east on Highway 202
to reach Tehachapi.

KEENE, CALIFORNIA

Out of Mojave I went along Silver Queen Road
and stopped to draw the Golden Queen Mine
sitting picturesquely on the side of Soledad
Mountain. Golden Queen was a gold mine
and later a silver mine, but all that was a
long time ago. It had'nt operated since
1941, however in 1976 the mine was
again put to work.
At the end of the Mojave-
Tropico Road is the Tropico Mine.
Gold was taken from the area
until 1956 when mining operations
came to a close.

GOLDEN QUEEN MINE, SOLEDAD MOUNTAIN

A retired "hard-rock" miner took me through
a portion of the Tropico. There are twelve
miles of tunnels! I looked down a 900 foot
shaft and tried to imagine what it would be
like to be a miner, and go to the bottom.
There was a wooden ladder, but my guide
said that most men rode down in the
big ore bucket. The tour ended
at the "glory hole", where the
vein had enlarged greatly.

TROPICO GOLD MINE ON THE HILL

SOME WILDFLOWERS
OF THE MOJAVE

PHACELIA

WILD MARIGOLD

DESERT MARIGOLD

The Grand Tehachapi Loop

One of the greatest accomplishments of railroad engineering, the Tehachapi Loop, can be seen from a vantage point along the Woodford-Tehachapi Road southeast of Woodford. The loop is a complete circle of a 3,795-foot circumference, which allows a train to gain 77 feet of altitude with a practical gradient up the steep Tehachapi Mountains. Completed in 1876, the loop was part of the solution to one of the principal barriers to the construction of a railroad over the Tehachapis—the steep ½-mile grade between the town of Caliente and the summit of Tehachapi, 14 straight-line miles away. The elaborate plan used the maximum gradients and the narrowest curves allowed by law. It winds 28 miles between the two towns, through a series of seventeen tunnels.

The Baker-Kelso Road across the Mojave

The trip begins on Interstate 15 and ends at Interstate 40 or eleven miles farther on the road to Amboy. From Baker the road stretches straight ahead and out of sight toward distant, rocky mountains.

I crossed a cattle guard in a few miles, and draped on a post nearby was a long-dead wildcat. I sketched flowers along the way. It is interesting how so many resemble snapdragons, lilies, marigolds, buttercups, and mustard, but with desert variations. You pass Joshuas and yuccas, then descend into a wide valley to view the spectacular Providence Mountains and the tiny railroad hamlet of Kelso at their base. Kelso has lawns and trees and a cavernous coffee shop where the cook, all in white, greeted me with a cool glass of fresh spring water. There are great mountains to see all the way to 40. The Granite Mountains must be one of nature's great sculptural masterpieces. Then there are the Marble Mountains, all purple, chocolate, and white, if you drive on toward Amboy.

FAMILY OF YUCCAS

GRANITE MOUNTAINS,
MOJAVE DESERT

THE PROVIDENCE MOUNTAINS
NEAR KELSO

In Kelso there are large palms and cottonwoods. The station itself is a grand and impressive place, in scale. Males can stay overnight in the hotel, but no ladies, I was told. I sketched as one of those long, long freight trains slowly and thunderously ground to a halt at my back.

UNION PACIFIC STATION, KELSO

Back Road through
the Panamint and Saline Valleys

Highway 395, north from San Bernardino, and 14, out of Mojave, head for the Panamint Valley. This is also the way to Death Valley. Saline Valley Road leaves Highway 190 farther north, somewhere between Panamint Springs and Keeler.

Twenty-one miles from Mojave you can turn off Highway 14 onto the Red Rock-Randsburg Road to see the old mining town of Randsburg. Near Johannesburg, close by is the Wildrose-Trona Road through Panamint Valley, with its vast views of desert and mountains. The peaks were rich with color and light in the setting sun. I drove past dry Searles Lake, a large chemical company, Trona and on down into the great Panamint Valley.

THE PANAMINT VALLEY

FIVE-STAMP MILL, RANDSBURG

Map labels:
BIG PINE
TO BISHOP
SALINE VALLEY
OWENS VALLEY
LONE PINE
KEELER
OWENS LAKE BED
190
190
PANAMINT SPRINGS
TO DEATH VALLEY
395
PANAMINT VALLEY
BALLARAT
WILDROSE-TRONA ROAD
178
TRONA
14
RED ROCK-RANDSBURG RD.
RANDSBURG
JOHANNESBURG
RED MOUNTAIN
MOJAVE
TO SAN BERNARDINO

SHEPARD'S STAGE COACH
ROAD ACROSS PANAMINT
VALLEY, BALLARAT

Before reaching Ballarat you can visit the Onyx Mine. Turn off at Nadeau Road for six miles. It is a four-mile dirt road diversion to Ballarat in Panamint Valley. I sketched the old General Store looking toward Shepard's Canyon across the valley. The scar of the stagecoach road that Mr. Shepard cut from Ballarat and Darwin Falls in the 1890's is still visible. The old schoolhouse is another of the few buildings still standing in the once bustling mining town. Boot Hill is there to see, Seldom Seen Slim having the most elegant headstone. His epitaph reads, "ME-LONELY? HELL, NO! I'M HALF COYOTE AND HALF WILD BURRO."

BALLARAT'S OLD SCHOOLHOUSE

When High and Dry Keeler was a Waterfront Town

It's hard to believe that at one time sleepy Keeler was a rip-roaring place with rows of saloons, a bustling Chinatown, and an honest-to-goodness waterfront. Both the Inyo and White mountains were once a miner's dream. Since the discovery of their mineral deposits in the early 1860's, untallied millions have been taken out in gold, silver, tungsten, marble, soda, and borax. In 1872 the lead and silver bars from Keeler's smelters were accumulating faster than they could be hauled around Owens Lake by freight wagon, so miners used them like bricks, to build shelters. The surplus was finally handled by construction of an 85-foot steamer that carried 70 tons of bullion a day across the 18 miles of blue water between Swansea and Cartago. Where a navigable Owens Lake lay before 1940, when the Los Angeles Aqueduct diverted its principal inlet, are today dazzling white salts. Busy, modern plants take borax and soda from the lake-bed deposits along U.S. 395, but on the 53-mile road that circles the lake there are stretches where the only evidence of the twentieth century is the paved road.

SALINE VALLEY

Saline Valley is uninhabited, so you will need plenty of gas and water for the 80-mile trip. The road is dirt for the most part. You will be astonished by the silent and somewhat forbidding desert landscape here. The only sound for me was the distant squawk of a big, western crow flying high above. There are many things to see, including the ruins of an old salt works, a salt lake, sand dunes, wild burros, and geologic formations of startling design, ending in a forest of piñon pine above the north end of the valley. I hope not too many people go through Saline Valley when you go, for the real pleasure was in being absolutely alone in such a vast and beautiful expanse of the earth's surface.

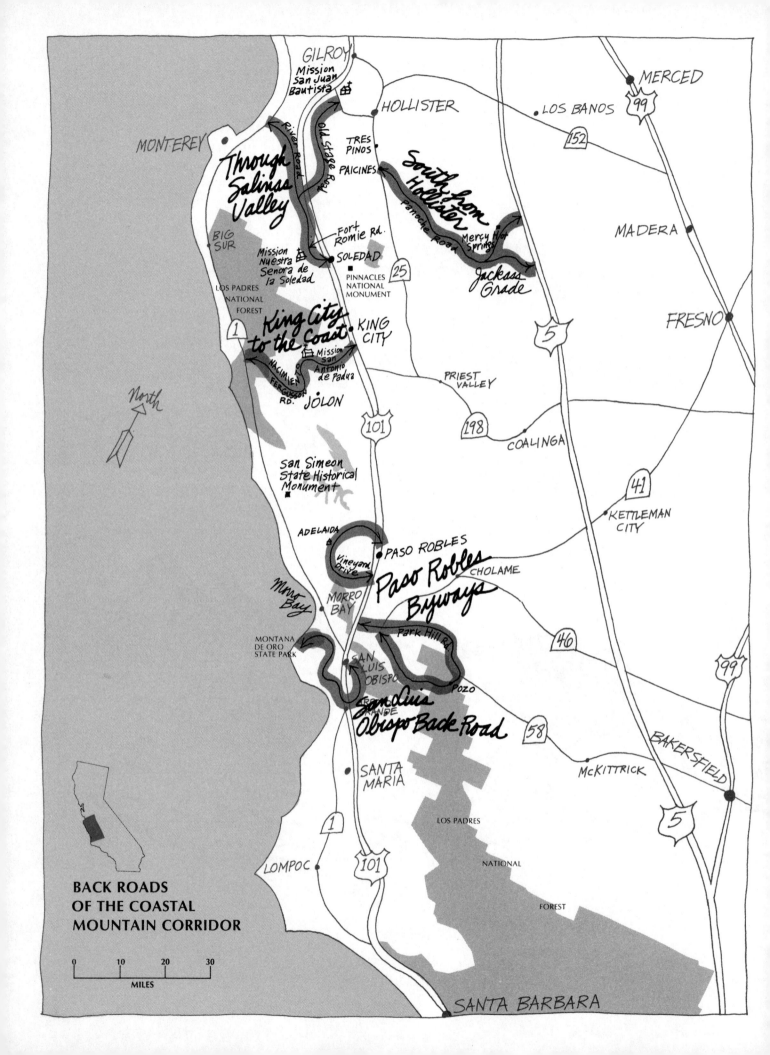

BACK ROADS
OF THE COASTAL
MOUNTAIN CORRIDOR

San Luis Obispo, Monterey, San Benito
Counties—Earthquake Country

THE COASTAL MOUNTAIN CORRIDOR

**The highway that hugs the coast between San Luis Obispo and Monterey, and
the fast freeway that parallels it farther inland, give access to roads that
wind through some of California's most dramatic ocean scenery, unspoiled
mountains, inland valleys, and agricultural land.**

State 1 twists above a rugged shore, often cloaked in fog or mist, where
cypresses cling to high bluffs and the ocean swirls over beaches or in and out
of rocky tide pools. On the inland side of the highway, a few unpaved roads
climb steeply into forested hills where deer and wild boar roam freely. Other
gravel or dirt roads follow ridgetops that offer views of ocean and mountains.
Between the Carmel-Monterey area at the north and San Simeon at the south,
the coast is wild, lonely, and windswept.

U.S. 101 takes an inland route, through the rich farmland of the Salinas
Valley. East and west of the freeway, quiet two-lane roads lead through
furrowed fields and crop lands into peaceful hills and valleys spread with
vineyards and orchards.

Early California history can be relived throughout this central coastal
region. In Monterey, one can stand at the edge of the bay claimed for Spain
by its discoverer, Juan Rodriguez Cabrillo, and visit restored buildings that are
reminders of the time when this city was first the Spanish and then the
Mexican capital of California. In San Juan Bautista, one can stand in the old
plaza where stagecoaches traveling between Monterey and the gold fields
rattled to a halt in the colorful days of the 1860's. Elsewhere in the coastal
mountains and valleys, one can stroll through gardens and cloisters of missions
founded by Franciscan padres some two centuries ago.

THE COAST SOUTH OF
MORRO BAY, MONTANA
DE ORO STATE PARK

San Luis Obispo Back Road

Not far from San Luis Obispo are the coastal bluffs of Montana de Oro State Park. Returning on Los Osos Road try Prefumo Canyon Road, just 1½ miles before reaching 101, for hills, farms, and views; then on to 101. Go east from Highway 101, at Pismo Beach, onto Hinds Avenue. Hinds becomes Price Canyon Road and goes to Edna Valley.

At Biddle Road I crossed the floor of the valley and going toward San Luis Obispo sketched that big bump in the landscape, Islay Hill. Approaching San Luis Obispo you will see housing developments marching up Los Osos Valley, houses taking the place of crops.

ISLAY HILL, CERRO SAN LUIS OBISPO AND BISHOP'S PEAK

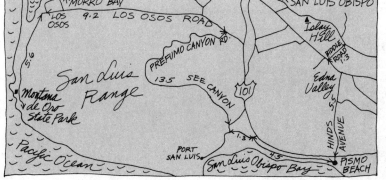

Byways East and West of Paso Robles

Five miles east of 101, on Highway 58, is Santa Margarita. Here is where the road to Pozo begins.

There's a 100-year-old saloon at Pozo with tractor seats for barstools. Continuing on Pozo Road, then Park Hill Road, I came across an incredible animal farm. Turkeys were gobbling, chickens cackling, ducks chasing ducks, geese honking, and all kinds of goats walking their new offspring. A shaggy, bearded Nubian goat nibbled the grass near my shoe. There were muddy, grunting pigs, bawling calves, braying donkeys, and horses and ponies!

ANIMAL FARM,
PARKHILL ROAD

THE FARMERS
CALL IT
"FIREWEED"

You'll enjoy traveling four roads to Adelaida:
Chimney Rock, Peachy Canyon, Vineyard,
and Adelaida. "People around here
don't pronounce the last "a" in Adelaida," said
the gas station attendant in Paso Robles.
This is barley country, but fireweed, the barley
farmer's enemy, bloomed orange in the farmlands.

FERMENTATION
VATS, WINERY
ROAD NEAR
TEMPLETON

Off Vineyard Road, near Templeton, there are redwood fermentation tanks at the old Rotta winery. Where the road from Adelaida comes into Nacimiento Lake Road there is "Chimney Rock" with great, steep sides and an eagle's nest on top. It is a most pleasant road to Adelaida, but there no longer is a town there!

EAGLE NEST ON
CHIMNEY ROCK

Quiet Route from King City to the Coast

Sulphur Springs Road to Mission San Antonio de Padua is through forests of oaks and, in springtime, meadows sprinkled with wildflowers. This landscape continues west on the Nacimiento-Fergusson Road, just south of the mission. Watch for cows and chipmunks! Then wind through Los Padres National Forest and down, down the truly exhilarating road to the sea.

ST. LUKE'S CHURCH, JOLON

MURAL TO TEACH
MUSIC TO INDIANS,
MISSION SAN ANTONIO
DE PADUA

THE PACIFIC COAST
FROM PLASKETT RIDGE

Off the Beaten Path: Mission San Antonio de Padua

The mission that graces the still-pastoral countryside near Jolon, southwest of King City, authentically duplicates the one that was constructed there between 1810 and 1813. To the traveler of today, remote Mission San Antonio de Padua is one of the most charming and interesting of the missions. In its prime, it was the home of some thirteen hundred Indians who tended crops and livestock and worked at various handicrafts. Here the men learned tanning, wine making, farming, building, and stock breeding. The women learned to cook, sew, spin, and weave. Water from the San Antonio River was channeled into an elaborate waterworks to operate the grist mill and to irrigate the fields. Though it is located in the midst of a military reservation criss-crossed with tank tracks, spacious Mission San Antonio de Padua offers more rewards to the traveler than perhaps any other of the California missions.

Another Way through Salinas Valley

Two miles south of Soledad, off Highway 101, the road leads to Soledad Mission

There are well-kept gardens at the Mission, and the old adobe ruins give atmosphere to the site.
This road gives splendid views of the agricultural Salinas Valley.

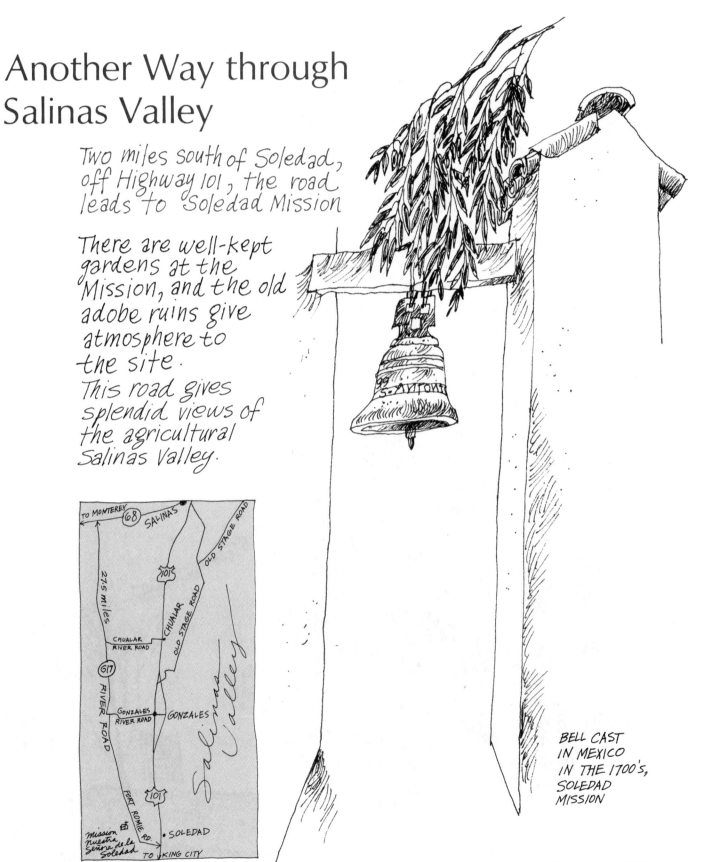

TO MONTEREY — 68 — SALINAS

OLD STAGE ROAD

101

27.5 miles

CHUALAR

OLD STAGE ROAD

CHUALAR RIVER ROAD

G17

RIVER ROAD

GONZALES RIVER ROAD — GONZALES

Salinas Valley

FORT ROMIE RD.

101

Mission Nuestra Señora de la Soledad

• SOLEDAD

TO KING CITY

BELL CAST IN MEXICO IN THE 1700's, SOLEDAD MISSION

You feel much closer to the land, especially after sitting on the ground in a broccoli field. I left River Road for Chualar and the Old Stage Road. The Stage Road wasn't through to San Juan Bautista, so I took the San Juan Grade Road over the mountain.

San Juan Bautista is a most pleasant place to visit, with its large Mission and other well-kept, old buildings surrounding the square. You will enjoy the ancient, gnarled pepper trees, the gardens, and the opportunity nearby to taste Almaden wines.

PEPPER TREE,
MISSION SAN JUAN
BAUTISTA

FARMING THE SALINAS VALLEY

BROCCOLI,
SALINAS VALLEY

South from Hollister
—A Back Road to Interstate 5

Hollister is 11 miles east of Highway 101 via either 156 or 25 farther north.

Santa Ana Road, out of Hollister, headed for green hills yellow with mustard flowers. I followed the road happily to Quien Sabe Road where I turned right. Coming out of the hills there is a picture-post-card view of the valley with the Immaculate Conception Church at its center.

SANTA ANA MOUNTAIN,
NEAR HOLLISTER

THE IMMACULATE CONCEPTION
CHURCH, NEAR TRES PIÑOS

Tres Piños, on Highway 25, has a bar dating back to 1883 and an old firehouse, among other items of interest. The boss at the Pinnacles Garage opened the firehouse doors for me so that I could sketch the Dodge firetruck.

The Rugged Rocks of Pinnacles National Monument

For travelers who enjoy hiking, rock climbing, picnicking, and camping, Pinnacles National Monument is an excellent destination for spring or fall. It is just off State Highway 25, 35 miles south of Hollister. It can also be reached via the steep, rutted Clear Creek Road, which climbs over the Call Mountains south of the New Idria Mine and then winds down to the Hernandez Valley and Highway 25. (Road conditions should be checked at the mine office before taking the Clear Creek Road.)

The spires and crags that rise above the canyon floors in Pinnacles National Monument are the result of weathering and erosion of massive lava flows that occurred 20 million years ago. Trails in the monument are in keeping with the fantastically carved and jumbled terrain. They include natural and artificial staircases, footholds and handholds cut into the rock, narrow wooden catwalks, vaulted passageways, crawl-through passages, and even a natural "castle" pierced by a 138-foot, man-made tunnel that opens abruptly onto a concrete bridge over a yawning "moat."

THE LITTLE RED FIREHOUSE
WITH WHITE TRIM, TRES PIÑOS

There are narrow and broad valleys, farms, cattle, and wildflowers to see, and in wide Panoche Valley only a cluster of deserted buildings remain of Panoche town itself. Two pigeon houses, a windmill, and other buildings still stand but the old dance hall pictured below has vanished!

COTTONWOOD TREE SEEDS

PANOCHE DANCE HALL AND BLACKSMITH SHOP

Panoche Road out of the Valley is a good dirt road, a bit steep at Jackass Grade, but passable and enjoyable in dry weather. Little Panoche Road past Mercey Hot Springs is an alternate route and is paved to Interstate 5.

VIEW FROM
JACKASS GRADE

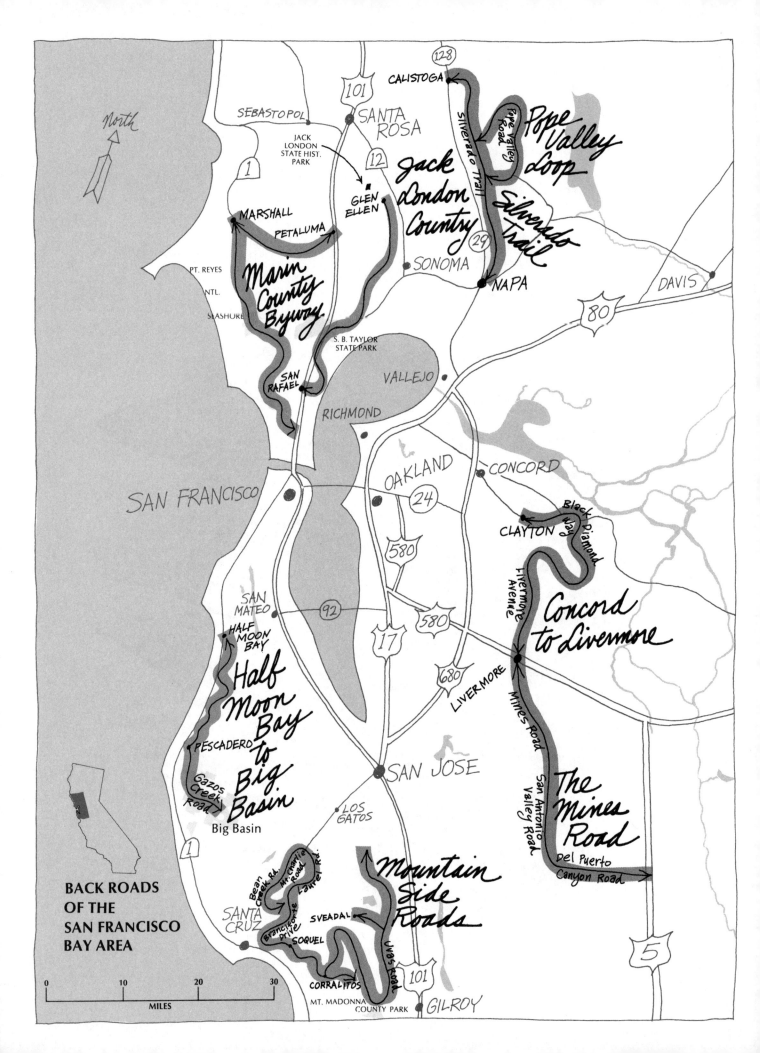

North

128
101
CALISTOGA

SEBASTOPOL
SANTA ROSA

1

JACK LONDON STATE HIST. PARK

GLEN ELLEN

MARSHALL
PETALUMA

12

Pope Valley Loop

Silverado Trail
Pope Valley Road

Jack London Country

Silverado Trail

SONOMA

29

NAPA

DAVIS

PT. REYES NTL. SEASHORE

Marin County Byway

80

S. B. TAYLOR STATE PARK

SAN RAFAEL

VALLEJO

RICHMOND

SAN FRANCISCO

OAKLAND

CONCORD

24

Black Diamond Way

CLAYTON

580

Concord to Livermore

Livermore Avenue

SAN MATEO

92

HALF MOON BAY

17

580

680

LIVERMORE

Half Moon Bay to Big Basin

Mines Road

PESCADERO

SAN JOSE

The Mines Road

Gazos Creek Road

Big Basin

LOS GATOS

San Antonio Valley Road

1

Del Puerto Canyon Road

Bean Creek Rd.
Mt. Charlie Road
Laurel Rd.

Mountain Side Roads

SANTA CRUZ

Branciforte Drive

SVEADAL

SOQUEL

Uvas Road

101

5

CORRALITOS

MT. MADONNA COUNTY PARK

GILROY

BACK ROADS OF THE SAN FRANCISCO BAY AREA

0   10   20   30
MILES

Wine Country—Marin and North Bay
Coastal and Mountain Byways

THE SAN FRANCISCO BAY AREA

**Developers are busy around San Francisco Bay, and metropolitan centers
continue to spread wider and climb higher. But beyond the subdivisions and
the city streets, back roads lead to rural areas where cattle graze on rolling
hillsides, farms survive, and vineyards glow red and gold in autumn.**

Five bridges span the Bay's waters, and many roads link the cities around its
edges and lead out from the Bay Area. State 1 winds north and south along
the ocean's shore. U.S. 101 follows the western edge of the Bay, and State 17
hugs the eastern shore. State 35 travels the forested spine of the peninsula
south of San Francisco. Interstate 80 and 580, and some less-traveled
highways, lead east to the cities of the Sacramento and San Joaquin valleys.

Though the peninsula to the south of San Francisco is well-blanketed with
civilization on its eastern side, winding roads explore the forested slopes of its
mountains and offer glimpses of ocean to the west. Behind the East Bay cities,
country lanes meander over the slopes of Mount Diablo and through countryside east of the mountain, where residential communities mix with walnut
orchards, dairy farms, and cattle ranches.

North of the Golden Gate, the water-oriented communities of the Marin
Peninsula attract residents and visitors in great numbers. High above them are
the wooded slopes of Mount Tamalpais. At the base of the mountain, sunlight
filters through a stand of virgin redwoods in Muir Woods National Monument.

In winter, migratory waterfowl gather on the shallow marshes of Bolinas
Lagoon. To the west, the grasslands of the Point Reyes Peninsula stretch away
to steep sea cliffs. Farther north, resorts border the Russian River. Traffic is
heavy here in summertime, but not far away on the rural roads are apple
country, dairy country, and wine country.

OLSSON OAK, SVEADAL

Santa Cruz Mountain Side Roads

This Santa Cruz mountain journey begins in Santa Clara County. South of San Jose, County Road G8, Almaden Expressway, brings you to McKean and then Uvas Road. West of Uvas Road, 4 miles on Croy Road takes you through the Swedish resort of Sveadal.

King Gustavus, and Louise, of Sweden had been here in 1926 upon the occasion of the dedication of this resort. Continuing on Uvas Road and on Watsonville Road one mile brings you to Kirigan Cellars. Originally this was Bonesio Winery. In 1964 Pietro Bonesio's concrete table was finally broken by the tree planted through its center. Friends had told him that it would happen, but Pietro said, " I will be dead by that time!" He wasn't. He died at 87 years of age, outliving his table by 3 years.

CONCRETE TABLE AND MULBERRY TREE, KIRIGAN CELLARS

Redwood Retreat Road, off Watsonville Road, leads to Mount Madonna Road and up the mountain to Mt. Madonna County Park. On the park grounds are the ruins of the turn-of-the-century millionaire's— Henry Miller—summer house. I sketched as 2 truant young boys climbed neighboring redwood trees. I heard one say,"Isn't this more educational than spending a day in that old school?"

RUINS OF HENRY MILLER'S
MOUNT MADONNA ESTATE

HAZEL DELL SCHOOLHOUSE (NOW DESERTED)

Mining Country: Quicksilver South of San Jose

Some of the oldest mining country in California lies at the eastern base of the Santa Cruz Mountains. The center of the area is the town of New Almaden, named for Almaden in south-central Spain. In this foothills region are pockets of rich, dark-red earth that the Indians called **moketka.** White men identified it as cinnabar. In 1824, nearly a quarter of a century before California's gold strike at Sutter's Mill, Don Antonio Suñol worked the moketka briefly, in the mistaken belief that it contained silver. He abandoned his efforts, and New Almaden drowsed until 1845 when Andres Castillero discovered that the red earth contained quicksilver. There were three mines in the Almaden area. The richest and most extensive was at Almaden itself, with more than 100 miles of tunnels honeycombing the red hills. Six miles north of New Almaden was Enriquita mine, named for the daughter of the mine manager. The Almaden and Enriquita together produced quicksilver valued at more than 50 million dollars. The Guadalupe mine, on the banks of the Guadalupe River, was less productive, chiefly because it was a difficult mine to keep dry.

APPLE TREE PRUNING,
COX ROAD

Coming down from Mt. Madonna and the Santa Cruz mountains, enjoyable roads to explore are Summit, Highland, Brown's Valley, Hazel Dell, Green Valley, Day Valley, Cox, Valencia School, and Trout Gulch roads.

I traveled along Highway 1, from Aptos, turning toward the mountains again on Branciforte Drive. Along here you can make an entertaining stop at "Mystery Spot." Granite Creek Road and Glenwood Drive bring you to Bean Creek Road, a most pleasant back road. It ends in Scotts Valley and a sea of glittering mobile homes.

North on Highway 17 I traveled east onto Laurel Road and Schultheis Road. I stopped to sketch a great pen of chickens, guinea hens, ducks, drakes, and geese. It was breeding season and there was much strutting, clucking, and chasing going on.

PRIVATE BRIDGE
ALONG BEAN CREEK ROAD

I showed my drawing to the family that owned the farm, and they knew each winged creature by name. I was flattered that I could have caught individual likenesses. From Schultheis Road you can turn right onto Woodwardia Highway, then left on Summit Road north, across Highway 17 to Mountain Charley Road.

HILLSIDE FARM, SCHULTHEIS ROAD

LOG CABIN,
MOUNTAIN CHARLEY ROAD

A sign at the entrance to
Mountain Charley Road says,
"An early pioneer toll road named
in honor of M.C. McKiernan who
survived a hand to hand battle
with a grizzly bear near here
on May 10, 1854 — speed limit —
20 mph — sound horn on blind curves"
I rode Mountain Charley at 10 mph,
or less. At the crest is an old
cabin made of logs. It is
supposed to be over 100 years old.
You exit onto Glenwood Drive,
not far from Highway 17.

South from Livermore along the Mines Road

Two miles south of Livermore, the Mines Road branches off Tesla Road. Upon reaching San Antonio Junction you may proceed toward Lick Observatory and San Jose, or go east along Del Puerto Canyon Road to Interstate 5.

I sketched at the 1883 Concannon Vineyards winery off Tesla Road. Wente Brothers Winery, another of California's fine, historic wine-making firms, is also nearby.

CONCANNON WINERY,
LIVERMORE VALLEY

THE "BRANDING
IRON", MINES ROAD

OAK
FIREWOOD
FOR SALE

ARROYO MOCHO,
MINES ROAD

At the "Branding Iron", Ruth, the co-owner, gave me
two brown eggs fresh from mother hen for my
breakfast. The grey cat rubbed against my leg as
I sketched. A mule nearby scratched loudly and
made undignified noises. In the morning, wildflowers
were out before this artist. There were dwarf
lupines, tidy tips, Indian paint brush, fragonia, and
goldfields, among others. Millions of flies gathered
around freshly splattered cow plops. These were
avoided. A drawing was made where dandelions
and buttercups grew in profusion along the
bed of the Arroyo Mocho stream.

CEDARS
AND DAVID'S CROSS,
FRANK RAINES COUNTY PARK,
DEL PUERTO CANYON ROAD

I left the Mines Road
for a less charming one, the
road toward Patterson. There were
great bushes of blue ceanothus
blooming on the precipitous hillsides.
It was the middle of the week, in
spring, and no one was at
Frank Raines County Park.... except me.

The Highest Road in the Bay Area

Southwest of Interstate 5/580, and continuing from Mines Road, sinuous San Antonio Valley Road follows the northern slopes of the Mount Hamilton Range, and opens to beautiful views of the valley of Arroyo Mocho. Just south of the Del Puerto Canyon Road junction, San Antonio Road turns west and becomes Bayou Road. It climbs through low-brush, scrub-grass cattle country, fed by several small, summer-dry creeks, to the 4,209-foot summit of Mount Hamilton. This is the highest road summit in the Bay Area. Atop the mountain is James Lick Observatory, open every Saturday and Sunday. Visitors can view the world's second-largest reflector telescope from a small gallery in the domed building that houses it, and then see the 36-inch refractor telescope in use since 1888. West of the summit, Mount Hamilton Drive winds for 19 panoramic miles down through wooded slopes of pine, oak, and manzanita, and past neatly manicured farms and apricot orchards, to Alum Rock Avenue in San Jose.

SOME BAY AREA WILDFLOWERS

MADRONE BERRIES

SELF-HEAL

MONKEY FLOWER

Back Road—Half Moon Bay to Big Basin

Higgins-Purisima Road begins a series of back road explorations off Highway 1. It starts 1 mile south of Half Moon Bay.

You travel past farms and cows and rolling hills, then turn sharply back where the valley has become narrow, and moist, and where suddenly there are redwoods, firs, and ferns. I reached Stage Road via Verde Road, Lobitos Creek Cutoff, Tunitas Creek Road, and Highway 1. Stage Road begins about a mile and a half south of Tunitas, through San Gregorio and across Highway 84. At Willowside Ranch begins the magnificent eucalyptus arcade. Stage Road ends at Pescadero and a short distance east of here is the road to Butano State Park.

EUCALYPTUS ARCADE,
STAGE ROAD

WHITEWASHED BARN
PURISIMA CREEK ROAD

STUMP ALONG
THE GAZOS

Redwood Parks in the Santa Cruz Mountains

Six parks in the Santa Cruz Mountains protect remnants of the primeval redwood forest that once extended from the southwest corner of Oregon all the way to the Santa Lucia Mountains south of Monterey. Big Basin Redwoods State Park (on State 236), established in 1901, is the oldest park in California's state park system. It encloses a handsome stand of mature trees, and its nature lodge has excellent exhibits. Portola State Park and San Mateo County Memorial Park (both west of State 35, Skyline Boulevard, and east of Big Basin), are popular day-use and camping parks. Henry Cowell Redwoods State Park (State 9, north of Santa Cruz) stretches for more than two miles along the San Lorenzo River. It is a day-use park, with 13 miles of trails. Butano State Park (east of State 1 and south of the town of Pescadero) and Forest of Nisene Marks State Park (north of State 1, just below Santa Cruz) can be used for hiking and for picnicking.

Leaving Butano State Park camping area on Gazos Creek Road a sign says "IMPASSABLE IN WET WEATHER." Douglas firs were the first big trees along this road. They dripped with lichen, especially the dead trees. Forest growth became more lush as I drove on. Red and white alders, maples, and redwoods made a dark, damp valley where ferns grew in abundance. Fourteen miles of narrow, winding road through thick forest ends at Big Basin Redwood State Park. The sign at this end of Gazos is more forbidding......"HAZARDOUS IN SUMMER, IMPASSABLE IN WINTER."

FOREST ALONG
GAZOS CREEK

BUCKEYE TREES,
BLACK DIAMOND WAY

The Long Way from Concord to Livermore

Concord to Clayton is 7 miles. Here you find the dirt road, Black Diamond Way. It connects with Nortonville and Kirker Pass roads to U.S. 4. Off Highway 4 at Antioch, Lone Tree Way, Empire Mine, Deer Valley, and Morgan Territory roads give glimpses of Mt. Diablo as they wend through canyons, meadows, and rolling hills.

There is a magnificent grove of California buckeye trees along Black Diamond Way. They grow on a steep hillside and the road passes among them. The buckeye seeds are as large as tennis balls and hang at the tips of branches. I stopped to sketch and to listen to the musical, crystal-clear songs of meadow larks. Occasionally one of those buckeye balls would drop with a "bonk" sound to the ground.

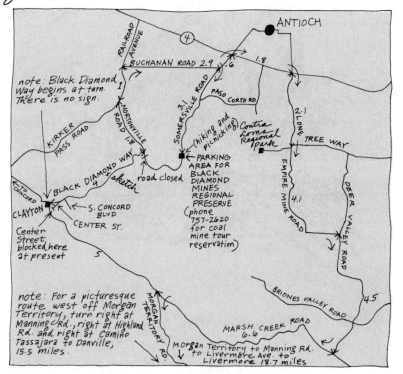

Marin County Byway

North of San Francisco, Highway 1 leaves 101 and in 3 or 4 miles you can turn off 1 onto Panoramic Highway.

Muir Woods and its magnificent redwoods are a 1 mile diversion. German-style Mountain Home is an inn farther along Panoramic. The Pacific Ocean is viewed to the west, and San Francisco Bay is to the south. Higher up still, on the way to Tamalpais Peak, is the great, stone Mountain Theatre where plays are performed each year in the open air. I drove on Ridgecrest with views of Bolinas Bay, then down to Alpine Lake, to Fairfax and Lagunitas.

MOUNTAIN HOME INN, PANORAMIC HIGHWAY

BOLINAS BAY

SOME WILDFLOWERS
OF NORTHERN CALIFORNIA

SILVERY WHITE
THISTLE, PURPLE
HEAD

WHITE LUPINE,
LAGUNITAS CREEK

BRIGHT YELLOW
MULE-EAR

Sir Francis Drake and the Indians

The Coast Miwok Indians considered the Point Reyes Peninsula the abode of the dead, but this didn't stop them from living there. Numerous mounds mark village sites, particularly along the shores of Tomales Bay where the villagers gathered the abundant shellfish. In 1578, Sir Francis Drake landed his ship, **Golden Hind,** in a place that sounds, in his chaplain's account, very much like Drake's Bay. The chaplain described "white bankes and cliffes," foggy weather, and moorlike land. Drake was met by Coast Miwoks and may have given them the Ming porcelains that have since been found in several village mounds.

MOUNTAIN THEATRE,
MT. TAMALPAIS

CURIOUS CATTLE
OF POINT REYES

All roads along the coast north of San
Francisco are picturesque. I drove Platform-
Bridge Road along Lagunitas Creek, the Pt. Reyes-
Petaluma Road, and Highway 1 north of Pt. Reyes
Station. I sketched cattle that came to
stare and chew, working quickly before they
returned to munch grass.

THE TOWN OF MARSHALL,
HIGHWAY 1

At the Marshall Boat Works, the commercial fishing boat "DONNA" was having its undersides painted as the owner discussed fishing successes with a fat fisherman friend. I sketched. The weather was sunny, the air fresh. A bank of fog was held back by the hills of Inverness across Tomales Bay. Turn right on the Marshall-Petaluma road for good views of the bay and the Pt. Reyes National Seashore area. Farther on there is a good view looking toward Petaluma with Hicks Valley below. This is sheep and cattle country and the hills roll along endlessly.

MARSHALL BOAT WORKS,
TOMALES BAY

HICKS VALLEY
MARSHALL-PETALUMA ROAD

San Rafael to Santa Rosa, via Jack London Country

My route was Mission San Rafael Archangel, San Rafael, as a starting point; then east along Pt. San Pedro Road, via 3rd Street, to China Camp, past Rat Rock to 101. The Black Point Cutoff, Lakeville Road, Stage Gulch Road, and Arnold Drive through the Valley of the Moon take you to Glen Ellen.

JACK LONDON'S GRAVE

Up the hill 1 mile is Jack London's place. Learn its history, then let the area's special beauty and mystique become a part of you. Discover the little graves of 2 children, near Jack's own lava gravestone. In his book "Burning Daylight" there is a description of them. Walk through the "Forest of Disappointment," and see traces of the old carriage road between his cottage and Wolf House.

TRACES OF THE OLD CARRIAGE ROAD, JACK LONDON STATE PARK

RUINS OF JACK LONDON'S WOLF HOUSE

Wine Country—The Silverado Trail

The easiest way to find the Trail is to go north of Napa on Highway 29 to Trancas Street, turn right, and in 2 miles go left onto Silverado Trail.

Here, before spring plowing, mustard flowers form a brilliant, yellow carpet amongst young vines. At Taplin Road, near St. Helena, is one of the original 60 or 70 stone bridges that caused this valley to be called "County of Bridges" in 1900. Opposite this stone bridge is an old schoolhouse painted dark green with white trim, the school bell still in its tower.

YOUNG VINEYARD ALONG THE SILVERADO TRAIL

STONE BRIDGE
AT TAPLIN ROAD

TO CALISTOGA

SILVERADO TRAIL

BIG RANCH ROAD

29

TRANCAS STREET
2

REDWOOD ROAD

MONTICELLO ROAD

HAGEN ROAD

City of Napa

TO 29

THE OLD SCHOOLHOUSE AT TAPLIN
ROAD AND SILVERADO TRAIL

Silver and quicksilver mining in the mountains north and east of the Napa Valley in the 1800's inspired the name of "Silverado," and in 1921 Silverado Trail officially got its title by a split three to two vote of the Napa Board of Supervisors. Until that time it was known as "The Old Back Road." The curves are continually being removed from the Silverado Trail, to my regret, thus encouraging motorists to speed, and pass all too quickly through an area of great beauty and interest.

THE NAPA RIVER
AT ZINFANDEL LANE

North of the Pope Street bridge you may turn right on Glass Mountain Road ½ mile to Glass Mountain Lane. Along the Lane is Elmshaven, the former home of Ellen G. White, respected 7th Day Adventist writer and leader. It is open for the public to see.
The trip was 30 miles from Napa to Calistoga. A mile or so farther north drive up Palisades Road or Old Toll Road for a close look at Calistoga's "High Rocks". Old Toll Road ends at Highway 29 on the way to Middletown.

ELMSHAVEN, 1885

"HIGH ROCKS,"
THE PALISADES RISE
ABOVE CALISTOGA

Napa Valley — A Perfect Place for a Honeymoon

Robert Louis Stevenson sojourned in the peace and quiet of northern California for nearly a year in 1879 and 1880. The Scottish writer married an American woman, and they honeymooned during the summer of 1880 in an abandoned bunkhouse of the defunct Silverado Mine on Mount St. Helena in the Napa Valley. In 1883 Stevenson celebrated that happy time in his book **The Silverado Squatters.** The author is remembered in St. Helena today in the Silverado Museum, at 1347 Railroad Avenue. Displaying only Stevenson memorabilia, the museum contains more than 1,500 artifacts including original manuscripts and letters, portraits and photographs of the writer, and even a desk he used when he lived in Samoa.

In St. Helena, on Highway 29, turn off at Madrona Street to Spring Mountain Road. This connects with Calistoga Road and Santa Rosa. High in the Mayacamas Mountains, 5½ miles from St. Helena, I sketched, looking eastward to the Napa Valley floor and the Howell mountains.

NAPA VALLEY,
FROM SPRING MOUNTAIN ROAD

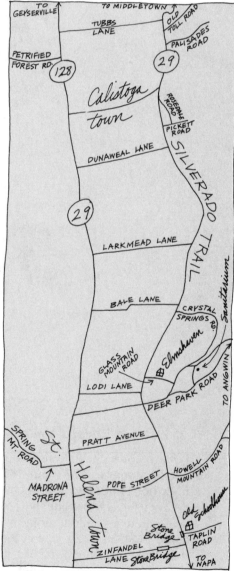

Pope Valley Loop

There are many roads into Pope Valley.
One is from Rutherford on Highway 29,
going east across Silverado Trail, to
Conn Dam, Hennessey Reservoir,
and through Chiles Valley.

POPE VALLEY STORE, 1913

BOILER AND PETUNIAS
POPE VALLEY WINERY

Several miles north of the Pope Valley Store is
Pope Valley Winery. It is built with timbers from
the old Oat Hill Quicksilver Mine and looks
much as it did when it was founded in 1910.

A bit farther north is Litto Damonte's place. Litto is a talented folk artist who works with old tires, washing machines, toilets, and other "found" objects, but most of all..... with hubcaps! He makes wishing wells and there are bird houses in profusion. You can see Litto's place from Pope Valley Road, but the permission of the owner would be required to view his art more closely.
You can return to Silverado Trail and Highway 29 via Ink Grade, or much more easily, over Howell Mountain Road past the 7th Day Adventist community of Angwin.

BIRD HOUSE AND TOILET SEAT PLANTER WITH HUB CAPS, LITTO'S PLACE

HUB CAP ARRANGEMENT, POPE VALLEY ROAD

TAHOE
NATIONAL
FOREST

GRASS VALLEY

RENO
80

49

Bypass to Tahoe

TRUCKEE

395

AUBURN
GEORGETOWN
WENTWORTH
SPRINGS
UNCLE
TOM'S

SACRAMENTO

80

50
FOLSOM

The Levee Road

Green Valley Road

COLOMA
PLACERVILLE
CAMINO

Lake Tahoe

50

FREEPORT

LOCKE

ELDORADO

NATIONAL

WALNUT GROVE

49

FIDDLETOWN
DAFFODIL HILL

FOREST

ISLETON

VOLCANO
RAILROAD FLAT

Gold Country
High Road

STOCKTON

SAN ANDREAS
MILTON

MURPHYS

4

TOIYABE

TRACY

4

ANGELS
CAMP

STANISLAUS
NATIONAL
FOREST

THE
ICEBERG
DARDANELLE

NATIONAL

FOREST

COPPEROPOLIS

Sonora
Pass

SONORA

MODESTO

BIG OAK
FLAT

High
Sierra
Loop

NEVADA

CALIFORNIA

North

BRIDGEPORT

99

120
Tioga
Pass

BODIE

167

YOSEMITE

LEE VINING

TOIYABE

MERCED

NATIONAL

PARK

NATIONAL

140

395

FOREST

Into Sierra National Forest

INYO

MADERA

145

AUBERRY
BIG
CREEK

NATIONAL

FRIANT

FOREST

INYO

168

DINKEY
CREEK

NATIONAL

FRESNO

TRIMMER

BISHOP

FOREST

SIERRA

**BACK ROADS OF THE CENTRAL
VALLEY AND THE SIERRA**

NATIONAL

FOREST

KINGS CANYON

NATIONAL

0   10   20   30

MILES

PARK

SEQUOIA
NATIONAL PARK

Side Roads West of State 99—The
Sacramento Delta—Gold Country

CENTRAL VALLEY AND THE SIERRA

Between the low mountains of California's coast ranges and the rugged granite peaks of the Sierra Nevada, the great Central Valley forms a tapestry of field crops, pasture lands, orchards, and residential areas. Arrow-straight roads crisscross fields of cotton and potatoes, onions and lettuce, tomatoes and rice.

California's two greatest rivers, the Sacramento and the San Joaquin, come together in a complex of sloughs that forms the Delta region. Here, fishermen try their luck, and cruisers, sailboats, and miscellaneous small craft nose about on the waterways. Sea-going freighters travel deep-water channels to inland ports at Sacramento and Stockton.

One of the most traveled routes between Northern and Southern California, State 99, heads up the east side of the Central Valley; Interstate 5 goes along the west side. Crossing the Valley, Interstate 80 and U.S. 50 connect the cities of the San Francisco Bay Area with the recreation areas in the Sierra Nevada and with cities on the east side of the range. They follow mountain passes along the two main emigrant routes taken by California's early settlers, and they intersect State Highway 49, which weaves its way through once-rowdy mining towns that sprang up across the Mother Lode in the 1850's. Weather and time have tumbled many of the gold-rush buildings. Some towns have disappeared completely in the path of progress and others have become thriving modern communities. Still others now drowse peacefully, surrounded by rolling hills.

East of the Gold Country, the slopes of the Sierra Nevada climb to majestic heights then drop off abruptly to desert-like countryside, where dusty roads lead to old mines in the mountains east of U.S. 395.

Fresno to Madera,
via Sierra National Forest

It is a roundabout 120-mile way between these two places, but most interesting. Highway 168 out of Fresno goes some 20 miles of the way. Where Toll House Road branches off, follow it another 6½ miles to Burrough Valley Road and the back roads.

Burrough Valley, Watts Valley, and Maxon roads bring you to Trimmer along the bank of Pine Flat Reservoir. I left Trimmer Springs Road to begin the dirt byway, Big Creek Road, on my winding way 29 miles to Dinkey Creek. The elevation gradually changed, and so did the temperature, from a hot 1,200-foot level at Pine Flat to a cool 6,000 feet near Dinkey Dome. You follow Big Creek for many miles, then circle past Cat's Head Mountain, Apperson Ridge, and Secata Ridge to get to where the tall pines grow.

BIG CREEK

FOOTHILLS OF THE SIERRA,
BURROUGH VALLEY ROAD

FENCE MEADOW LOOKOUT,
ELEVATION 5256 FEET

APPERSON RIDGE,
PINE FLAT RESERVOIR
ON THE LEFT

I visited the lookout at Fence Meadow. Two tiny dogs barked at me with high, piping barks from their perch atop the lookout tower. The lookout told them to be quiet and yelled to me, "Come on up." He opened a trap door, and I climbed the steep two flights to his room with view all around. "It's become so hazy," the lookout said, "I haven't seen the coastal range from here for 6 years. It gets worse every year and some day it won't do any good to have a fire lookout!"

I stopped at Nutmeg Springs. You can follow it to its source 100 feet from the road, where it bubbles from the ground beneath trees and rocks. And one of the trees is a California nutmeg!

Upon reaching Dinkey Creek Road I drove to Mckinley Sequoia Grove to draw one of the immense trees. A section of trunk was all that I could manage.

The Dinkey Creek Bridge is a satisfying piece of engineering to study. People enjoy fishing near the bridge, walking over it, and looking down and around..... and, of course, artists sketch it occasionally. Dinkey Road goes past big trees, meadows, and stretches of granite rocks. Wildflowers are abundant, especially the magnificent purple mountain lupine. I sat to sketch a pine tree, but got so bitten by red ants I had to stand to finish the drawing, and there were pesky flies that seemed to be playing a game of "catch-me-if-you-can." They _know_ you cannot catch them, however, so it's not fair!

DINKEY CREEK BRIDGE

CONES AND PINE,
DINKEY CREEK ROAD

148

BALD MOUNTAIN,
DINKEY CREEK ROAD

The Big, Big Trees of the Sierra Nevada

The world's largest living things, the Big Trees of the Sierra Nevada (**Sequoiadendron giganteum**), occur in groves along a 250-mile range on the west slopes of the Sierra Nevada. The discovery of these giants is generally credited to the members of the Joseph R. Walker exploration party which crossed the Sierra in 1833, but the trees did not come to the attention of the public until 1852, when the Calaveras Grove was discovered by a hunter named A. T. Dowd, who accidentally came across it while pursuing a bear. Largest of the giants is the General Sherman Tree in Sequoia National Park. It has an incredible height of 272 feet, a diameter of 30 feet at chest level, and a total trunk volume of about 50,000 cubic feet. Oldest is the Grizzly Giant in Yosemite National Park; its age is estimated at 2,700 years.

HUNTINGTON LAKE

Off Dinkey Creek road you can take Highway 168 past Shaver and Huntington lakes, where people come by the thousands during the summer to escape the heat of the San Joaquin Valley and to boat, bathe, fish, and camp. There are tamarack trees and white firs growing at the 7000-foot elevation around Lake Huntington. I chose to take Huntington Lake Road down the mountain to Big Creek. This is a winding road with deep views into the valleys. At Big Creek I sketched the big pipes called penstocks, and the "Kerckhoff Dome." The penstocks carry water from Huntington Lake into the big power house and move the turbines to make as many as 81,000 kilowatts, if called for. I bought some "grape-ade" children were selling along the road. It was terrible. I told them to add more flavoring and more ice! The Auberry Road 6 miles below Shaver Lake Heights eventually connects with Millerton Road, Friant, then on to Madera via Highway 145.

THE PENSTOCKS AND
KERCKHOFF DOME,
NEAR BIG CREEK

Interstate 80 Bypass on the Way to Tahoe

Highway 49 leaves Interstate 80 at Auburn. At Cool you can turn onto the Georgetown Road, Highway 193, to Georgetown.

At Greenwood I sketched a 1934 Ford V-8 fire truck, ready for action, parked on the porch of an ancient dwelling. Now the village has its own diminutive Fire Department building.

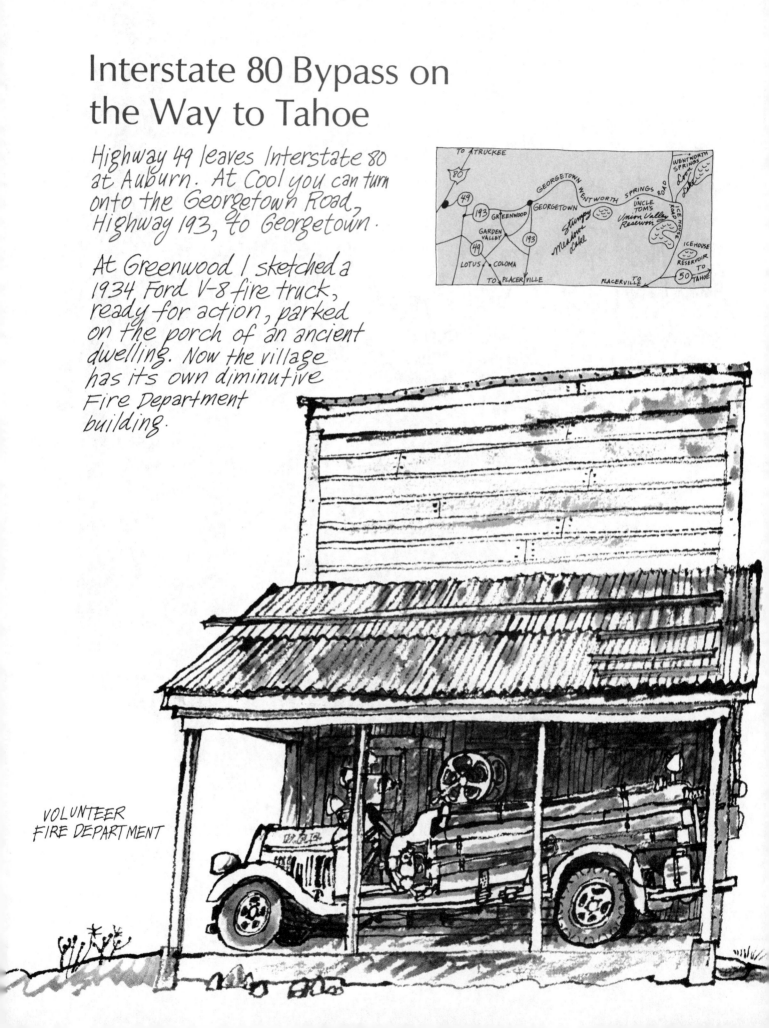

VOLUNTEER FIRE DEPARTMENT

Living Memories of the Glitter of Gold

Yankee California had its real beginning in Coloma early in 1848 when James Marshall saw a glitter of gold in the millrace of John Sutter's sawmill. In January of 1848, when Marshall made his discovery, California had about 15,000 inhabitants. Two years later there were 92,000, nearly two-thirds of them in full-time pursuit of the yellow metal. Placerville was once one of the great camps of the Gold Country. Georgetown's streets were lined with miners' shacks and canvas meeting halls. Garden Valley began life as a mining camp called Johnstown, was renamed when its residents turned to truck farming. Greenwood was established by a trapper and his two sons as a supply center for the miners.

There were 3,000 souls in Georgetown in 1854. Most are now memorialized in the large cemetery.

LOG BUILDING AT UNCLE TOM'S

East of Georgetown, stop at the Ranger Station in Buckeye for an Eldorado National Forest map and the latest road information. Stumpy Meadows Lake has a good campground. East toward Uncle Tom's the road eventually becomes dirt.

In the 1800's a black trapper named Uncle Tom opened up this forest area and until recently the Lawyer family lived here. The place has a mysterious atmosphere of the past, with its ancient cedar trees and old wooden buildings. A dirt road continues from here to Loon Lake Road.

LOON LAKE,
SACRAMENTO'S WATER SUPPLY

Although it has a new metal roof, the old Wentworth Springs stage coach stop has deteriorated considerably. It is a location of great beauty. High rocks form a backdrop to the ghostly old hotel, and a sparkling brook is in the close foreground.

Lawyer Cow Camp can be reached by passenger car, but Wentworth Springs must be hiked to or would require the use of a jeep or pickup.

THE OLD STAGE COACH HOTEL
AT WENTWORTH SPRINGS

KEYSTONE LODGE #161,
MILTON

High Sierra Loop

Twenty-five miles east of Stockton, County Road J14 goes 7 miles to Milton. This began the "High Sierra Loop."

Milton is distinguished only by a huge building, for Milton, that is: Keystone Lodge #161, moved from Copperopolis in 1881. Milton was then a railroad stop between Copperopolis and the city of Stockton, and a more industrious future was predicted for it at that time. Hunt Road begins here and rolls and wanders pleasantly to Copperopolis.

EARL THOLLANDER

VIEW FROM O'BYRNES FERRY ROAD BRIDGE

SOME MOUNTAIN WILDFLOWERS

SCARLET
MONKEY FLOWER

WHITE AND BRIGHT
YELLOW LOTUS

MEADOW
MONKEY FLOWER

THE DARDANELLES,
FROM DONNELLS OVERLOOK

O'Byrnes Ferry Road meets 108,
a fast highway to the top of the
Sierra, via Sonora. You can
explore Hell's Half Acre Road, just
beyond Strawberry, but get a
map first at the Ranger Station
in Pinecrest. At Donnells
Overlook, farther along on 108, is
a dramatic view to the deep
canyon below, and Donnells Reservoir.
From here I sketched the
Dardanelles with 8 to 10,000-
foot-high crags and buttes.

PONDEROSA PINE,
HELL'S HALF
ACRE ROAD

161

"THE ICEBERG,"
CLARK FORK ROAD

162

I turned off 108 onto the Clark Fork Road, which follows a clear mountain stream running through this glaciated valley. I was most curious about "The Iceberg," so-called on my map. No one could be disappointed in viewing this impressive 8,000-foot chunk of granite. From Sonora Pass, farther along 108, you can see Leavitt Peak towering at 11,570 feet. I sat at the foot of a gnarled pine and sketched, brushing away biting flies.

LEAVITT PEAK, SONORA PASS

THE GHOST TOWN OF BODIE

Down from the high Sierra to
Highway 395 and Bridgeport, a lively
tourist town, I traveled farther to
turn onto dusty Bodie Road. Bodie is a
ghost town with more structures preserved
than is usual. Try to be there before the
other tourists arrive, to feel the ghosts
moving about. Take Cottonwood Canyon Road
out of Bodie past weird Mono Lake, then
up over Tioga Pass from Lee Vining.

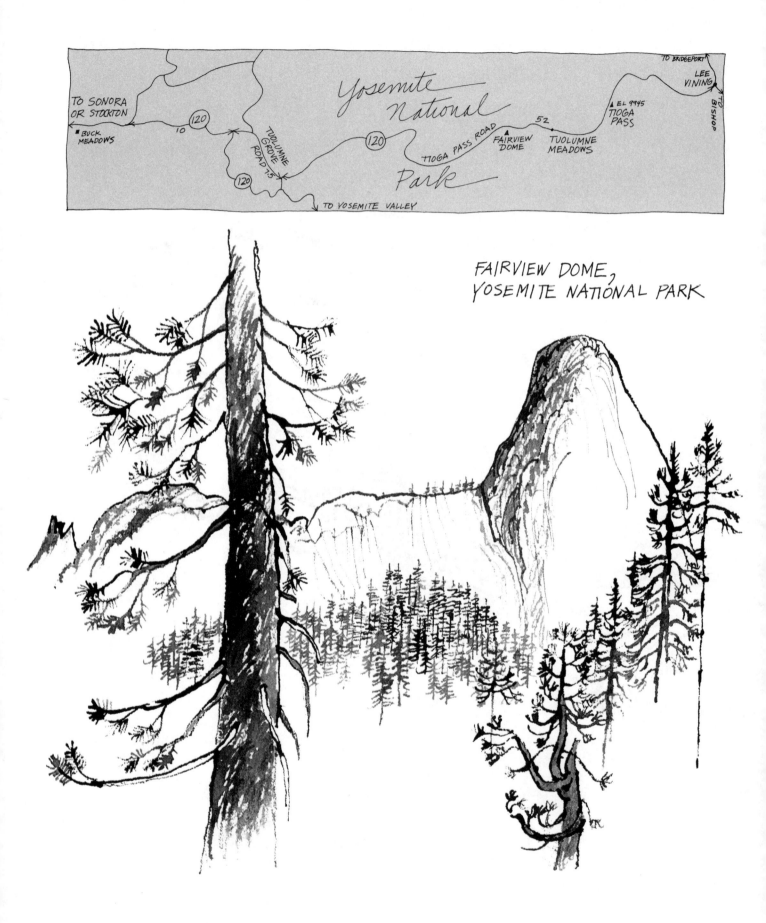

TO SONORA
OR STOCKTON

BUCK
MEADOWS

10

120

TUOLUMNE
GROVE
ROAD 1-5

120

TO YOSEMITE VALLEY

Yosemite
National

Park

120

TIOGA PASS ROAD

FAIRVIEW
DOME

52

TUOLUMNE
MEADOWS

EL 9945
TIOGA
PASS

TO BRIDGEPORT

LEE
VINING

TO
BISHOP

FAIRVIEW DOME,
YOSEMITE NATIONAL PARK

From my camping place along Highway 120 in Yosemite National Park, I began a sketch of Fairview Dome. The mosquitos literally drove me into the camper, so I waited until the following morning and completed the drawing while the bothersome insects were still frozen stiff. My fingertips were somewhat frozen, too. Forty-six miles from Tioga Pass you can take Tuolumne Grove Road through a great forest of uncut sugar pine and a grove of giant sequoia. You can drive through "Dead Giant", too, if you're not too big.
At the bottom of the Tuolumne Grove Road is Highway 120 to Sonora and points west.

GIANT SEQUOIA,
TUOLUMNE GROVE ROAD

APPLE ORCHARD,
CAMINO

Gold Country High Road

Just 7 miles beyond Placerville, off Highway 50, is the apple and cider town of Camino. The gold country journey begins with the true gold of Apples.

It is a good idea to get a brochure and map of the area from one of the growers. Mine was obtained at Larson Barn. I stopped to sketch at one ranch where the grower was desperately trying to pick his apples before they fell to the ground and were bruised. He was a little late, for this artist was surrounded by a "Golden Delicious" carpet of gold and green. I could not step without making applesauce. From here, country roads travel to Pleasant Valley, Aukum, Fair Play, and River Pines. Just before turning to Fiddletown, visit the D'Agostini Winery, founded in 1856.

D'AGOSTINI WINERY

THE WAR LORD, CHOW...
DR. YEE'S HERB SHOP,
FIDDLETOWN

Fiddletown has a small museum perhaps
unequaled in California for authentic historical
atmosphere. It is Dr. Yee's Chinese Herb Shop.
It seems as if nothing within its 2½-foot walls
of "rammed earth" has been disturbed since the
1800's, including the opium den.
The museum is generally open on weekends
or by special appointment.
When in Fiddletown, note the incredible fiddle
atop the community Hall.

FIDDLETOWN COMMUNITY HALL

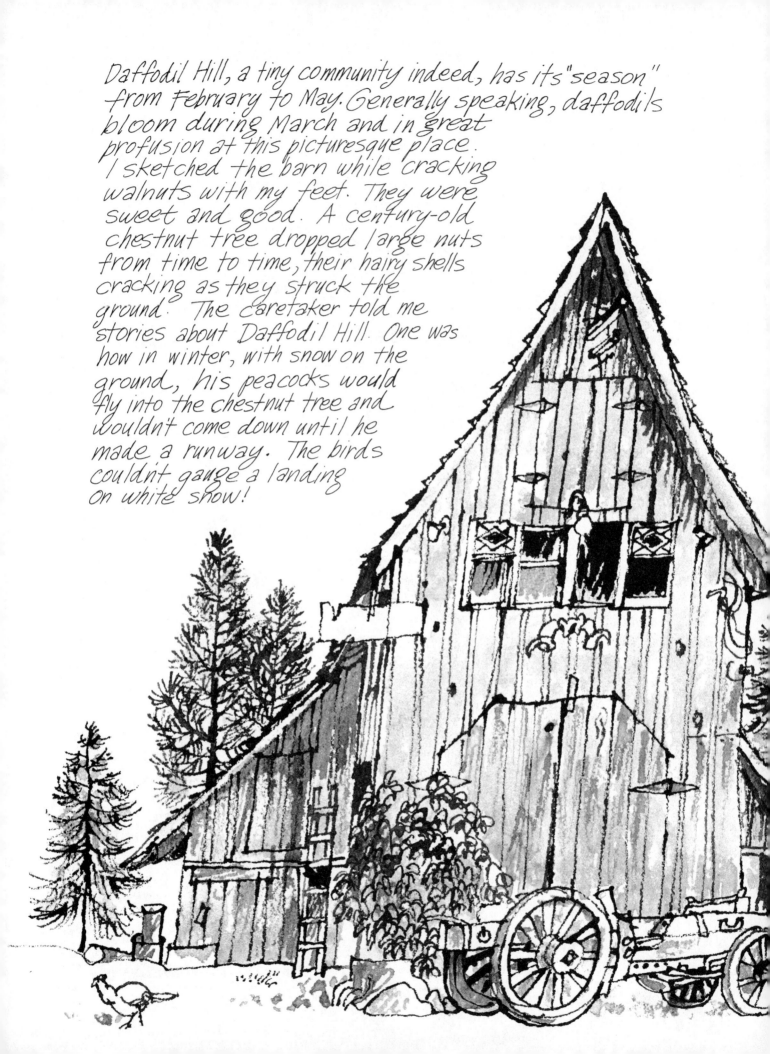

Daffodil Hill, a tiny community indeed, has its "season" from February to May. Generally speaking, daffodils bloom during March and in great profusion at this picturesque place. I sketched the barn while cracking walnuts with my feet. They were sweet and good. A century-old chestnut tree dropped large nuts from time to time, their hairy shells cracking as they struck the ground. The caretaker told me stories about Daffodil Hill. One was how in winter, with snow on the ground, his peacocks would fly into the chestnut tree and wouldn't come down until he made a runway. The birds couldn't gauge a landing on white snow!

Three miles down Daffodil Hill is the historic
town of Volcano, and this entrance to the
community is particularly pleasant. It was
autumn and the yellow leaves of locust trees
fluttered in the air. Once upon a time there
were 17 hotels and 37 bars here and it could
boast being the largest city in California!
Masonic Cave, just outside Volcano, is formed
of blue stone and is covered with thick moss.
The path to the cave was strewn with yellow
and orange maple leaves.

DAFFODIL HILL BARN, 1894

THE OLD ASSAY OFFICE, VOLCANO

"CHAW SE,"
INDIAN GRINDING ROCK,
VOLCANO

Miwok Mortars: An Outdoor Indian Kitchen

Within the boundaries of Indian Grinding Rock State Historical Monument near Volcano is the largest bedrock mortar ever found in the western United States. Scattered over a 7,700-square-foot limestone outcropping in the 40-acre park are 1,158 mortar holes and 363 petroglyph designs. Before the Gold Rush, Miwok Indians met here in the fall when the acorns were ripe (from middens and artifacts discovered, it is surmised that many Indians lived here all year). Using the rock, and stone pestles, they ground nuts, berries, and seeds into palatable food. Because of the geological and historical interest of the rock, a replica is in the Smithsonian Institution in Washington, D.C.

Railroad Flat was named for the primitive mule train ore cars used at the "Petticoat Mine". The general store is still in business, although the town has disappeared. The hall above the store was rented to the IOOF in the early days.

THE GENERAL STORE, 1867, RAILROAD FLAT

You can investigate Mountain Ranch, Sheep Ranch, and Mercer Cave (there is a fee charged for a visit to the cave) before arriving in the attractive town of Murphys to complete this gold country high road.

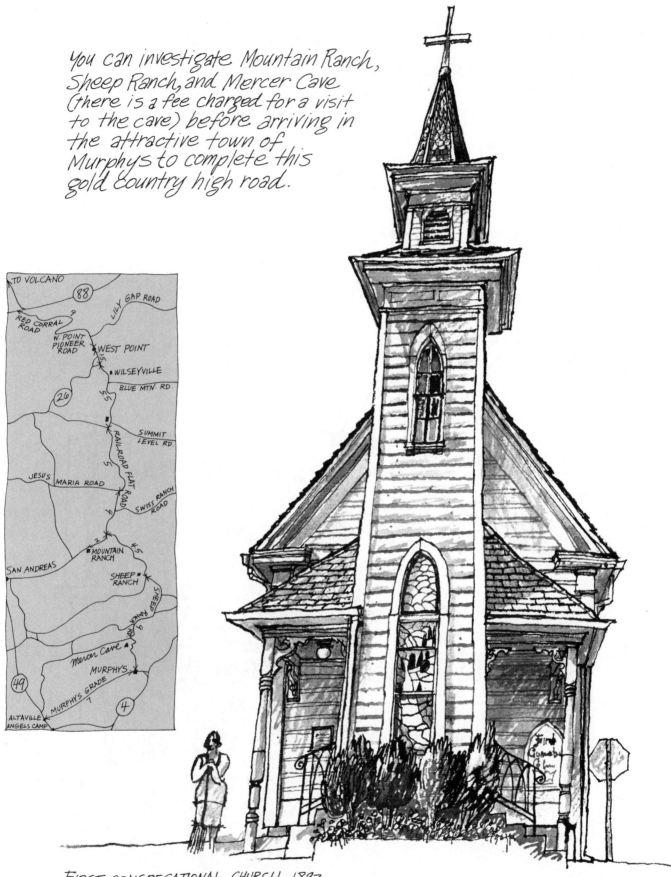

FIRST CONGREGATIONAL CHURCH, 1897
MURPHYS

South from Sacramento along the Levee Road

Approaching Sacramento from the west on Interstate 80, you turn off at Jefferson Boulevard, then Gregory Avenue to South River Road. You are now on the levee.

The Sacramento River is on your left, and below you, on the right, is the vast farming area of the delta. Pretty country towns along the way are Clarksburg and Courtland. At Locke the experience is varied indeed. This is a town created in 1913 by Chinese merchants. It boomed, then vegetated. It is still vegetating; however, in very few places in California can one feel in touch with the past as in Locke. A movie had been filmed recently in Walnut Grove, and my sketch included some of the atmosphere created by set designers. Visit Isleton next. You are now on Highway 160.

ONCE UPON A TIME THERE WA THE "STAR THEATRE" LOCKE

EDDIE'S,
WALNUT GROVE

THE EAST GATE,
FOLSOM PRISON

The Green Valley Road
from Folsom to Placerville

Natoma Street, out of Folsom, becomes Green Valley Road, which runs 25, or so, miles to Placerville.

You may drive to the prison, off Green Valley Road, to visit its handicraft shop and see the massive East Gate. Along Deer Valley Road you will pass the 1871 adobe Jacob Zentgraf house. I visited the Zentgraf family cemetery on Starbuck Road. There lie John, Frank, Lambert, William, Jacob Jr., Gabriel, Jacob Sr., his wife, and two without headstones. Jacob outlived them all. An older resident I spoke to said that Jacob Zentgraf gave his boys a bottle of home-made "grappa" every day. That was the reason for their early demise, I was told. Jacob lived to be 89, however, and I'm sure he didn't pass up the grappa. At Jay Hawk Cemetery birds sang in the cypress trees, cowbells tinkled from over the hill, wind whistled eerily in the hollow metal pipes holding up the cemetery sign. Deer Valley Road returns to Green Valley Road at Rescue.

JAY HAWK CEMETERY, DEER VALLEY ROAD

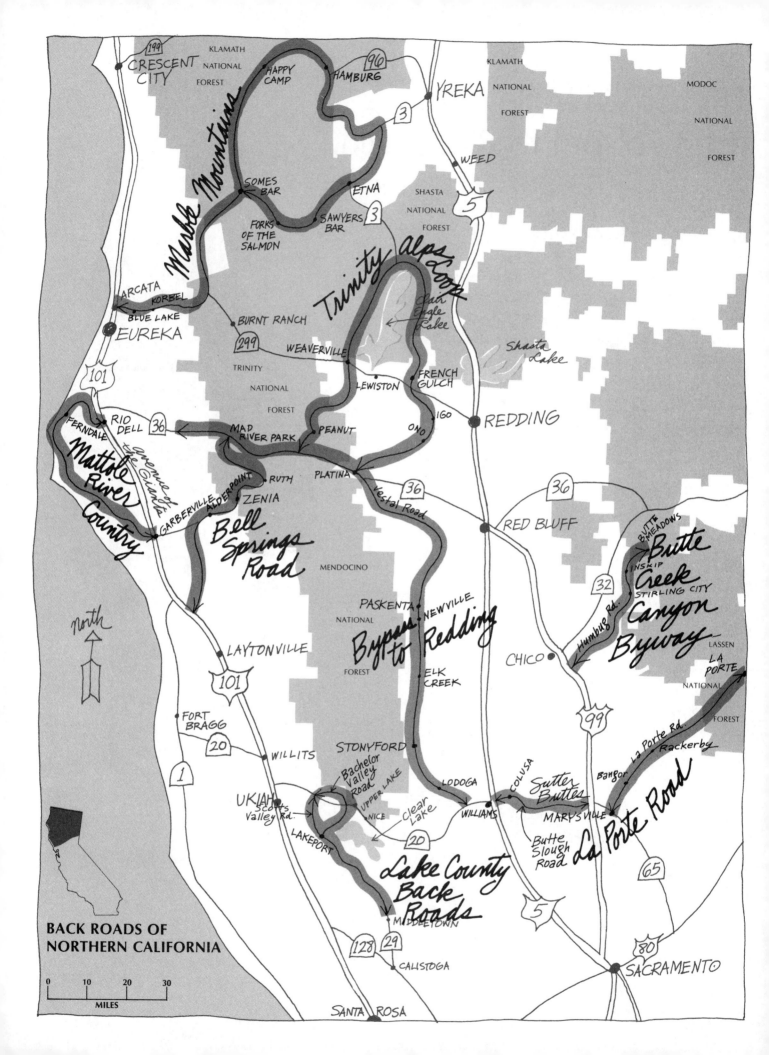

BACK ROADS OF
NORTHERN CALIFORNIA

Trinity Alps—The Humboldt Coast
Coastal Mountain Byways

EXPLORING NORTHERN CALIFORNIA

Across the northernmost portion of California, a varied terrain awaits the back roads explorer. Away from the freeways, this is a lonely land. Fog shrouds beaches tucked between grassy headlands, bluffs rise above booming breakers, redwood groves shelter a multitude of wildlife in parks that protect the tallest trees on earth.

In Northern California, a few easily accessible lakes and gigantic reservoirs lure boaters, water skiers, swimmers, and sightseers. Elsewhere, clear pools and sun-dappled meadows are tucked into mountain vastnesses where trails offer escape from the sights and sounds of civilization.

Three major highways speed traffic in a north-south direction through this part of California, skirting the edges of the quiet country that the back roads reach. Interstate 5, which cuts a swath through the center of the state, crosses Shasta Lake and passes in the shadow of Mount Shasta's snow-capped peak. At the western edge of the state, U.S. 101 follows a winding route through the redwood country and gives access to forest parks and seacoast views. Far to the east, U.S. 395 parallels the California-Nevada border and traverses a completely different landscape of irrigated pastures and open range land, where barns and farmhouses nestle in valleys between sage and juniper-cloaked hillsides.

Connecting these busy freeways, a scattering of state highways reaches east and west: to the resort areas around Clear Lake, to once-lively Gold Rush towns in the Trinity country, through the deep canyon of the North Fork of the Feather River, to Lassen Volcanic National Park. These roads give access to other roads, sometimes gravel or dirt—the back roads that explore lofty peaks, or follow the banks of tiny creeks, or wind through meadows colorful with wildflowers after winter rains.

All of the north-south routes in the upper part of the state are intersected by State 299, which runs east from Arcata, on the coast, to Cedarville and the Nevada border.

Lake County Back Roads

Highway 20 travels the north east shore of Clear Lake through Nice and Upper Lake. Beyond the latter, Witter Springs Road will take you to Bachelor Valley.

I would rather call it "Valley of the Barns". Because there are so many along the back roads, I have tried to avoid sketching barns, but those in this area are irresistible.

On Hendricks Road, off Scotts Valley Road, is a barn with so many woodpecker holes the beams look like filigree.

BACHELOR'S VALLEY BARN

SCOTTS VALLEY
WOODPECKER BARN

Clear Lake's Bloody Island

Before the white men came to Clear Lake to enjoy the hot springs, the mineral waters, and the abundance of fish, Pomo Indians roamed the countryside around the lake. They wove canoes from the tules that grew along the shore; they lived on fish from the lake, and seeds as well as berries and fruits from the land. Fur trappers arrived in the early 1800's, and they were followed by cattlemen. Cruel treatment of the Indians by two settlers, Andrew Kelsey and Charles Stone, resulted in the deaths of the two men in 1849 and a subsequent bloody massacre of Pomos by the soldiers who retaliated. The Indians were rounded up on a small island at the north end of the lake. More than 100 Pomo men, women, and children were killed, and the island became known as Bloody Island.

East from Marysville along the La Porte Road

From Colusa (west of Marysville), take Butte Slough Road, Pass Road, and Butte House Road past interesting "Sutter Buttes." Return to Highway 20 to Marysville and follow Highway 70 to Woodruff Lane, then Mathews Lane and Ramirez Road to La Porte Road.

SUTTER BUTTES

Past Bangor, and on the way to Rackerby, was a rock with religious slogans printed on it. I was traveling with another artist and you see him "immortalized" in the drawing below. He's sketching the message on the other side of the rock.
Towns along La Porte Road were stage coach stops in the early days of mining. Paul Rackerby is dead but remnants of his town remain.

PREPARE
TO MEET
THY GOD

This was rolling foothill country and a distant graveyard on a hill attracted my attention. I walked there to sketch while cattle stopped their grazing to watch.

L.A. SQUIRES.
BORN. 1857.
12·25·
DIED·1916
1·25·
AGE·58·
AT REST.

GRAVEYARD ON THE HILL,
LA PORTE ROAD, THIS
SIDE OF BANGOR

In Rackerby I sketched Clarence Day sitting on the porch of his 100-year-old home, "built with sluice-box and flume lumber," he said. Clarence smoked cigarettes and told me stories about his life, while I sat in the shade of his black walnut tree and worked. He told me details of the 1927 blizzard in Oklahoma and about the time he drove an axe into his foot. Being "stove up" at his lumbering trade, he had to supplement his social security income by salvaging junk. He used old bedsteads for fences and gates around the house. I was completing my drawing when Day's 14-year-old horse came along for morning "carrot time." Clarence and his horse are now dead but the property, owned by brother Jim, is much as it was then. At Strawberry Valley is a store built in 1853. The owner had collected 52,032 beer can tabs and strung them together decoratively as a solution to the litter disposition problem in front of his grocery store. La Porte was called "Rabbit Creek" in 1850 at the time of the discovery of gold; however, in 1857 the more distinguished name of "La Porte" was given to the town.

CLARENCE DAY OF RACKERBY, LA PORTE ROAD

Butte Creek Canyon
Byway out of Chico

Humbug Road branches off
of Skyway, the road to
Paradise, a few miles
east of Chico and
Highway 99.

HONEY RUN COVERED BRIDGE

Humbug Road goes by a shady cemetery near Centerville, a tiny community, and climbs up and up to Skyway Road and 3000-foot-high Stirling City. I sketched Red Keller's woodpile on the main street. Along came Red as the drawing was being completed. He barked in a gruff voice, after taking a look, "If I could get that drawing I'd send it to my maw and she'd jump in the air and kick her heels four times before she came down.... and she's 84!"
Out of Stirling City you climb past tall timber country to Inskip. The Inn there is a former stage coach hotel, the only one left of the 5 that once were in business.

ARMY SPACE HEATER, INSKIP INN

RED'S WOODPILE,
STIRLING CITY

Bull Hill Road goes to Butte Meadows
and Humboldt Road to Jonesville, where
an old hotel and stage coach barn still
stand. You can reach Lake Almanor
from here, if the snow has melted
(I couldn't make it in April), or return
to Butte Meadows and Lomo on
Highway 32 to Chico.

Interstate 5 Bypass to Redding

From Williams on Interstate 5, Highway 20 will lead you to King and Leesville roads for the back road trip north to Stonyford, Elk Creek, Newville, and Paskenta.

A long-time-dead coyote was strung on a post. Rugged looking Hereford bulls watched as I sketched it. In the distance turkey buzzards sat silently on the branch of a dead tree, crickets and birds sang. Poor, rotting coyote!

ANCIENT CYPRESS, ELK CREEK CEMETERY

Roads to the Past and the Present in the North Country

The gold rush that took place in California's northern Coast Ranges was never as well chronicled as mining in the Mother Lode, yet many millions of dollars in mineral wealth were extracted in the 1850's. Until the California and Oregon Railroad reached Redding in 1872, Shasta was the important city of the north country. Today, Shasta's main street is a historic monument where the façades of old brick buildings speak of the prosperous past. West from Shasta, State 299 parallels the old Trinity Trail, famous in turn as an Indian path, a pioneer trail, and a gold rush wagon road. State 3 to the north was once part of the old California-Oregon Wagon Road, the main route north from Shasta to Callahan and Yreka. Trails laid down originally by miners, prospectors, and cattlemen crisscross the roadless wilderness of the Marble, Salmon, Trinity, and Yolla Bolly mountains. State 96, which skirts the west side of the Salmon Mountains, follows the twisting Klamath River, where many communities that began life as mining camps now cater to droves of enthusiastic fishermen, who come here for some of the best steelhead fishing in the state.

ABANDONED MILSAP HOME, NEWVILLE

HONEY BEE FEEDERS,
GARLAND ROAD TO PASKENTA

A series of roads brings you to
Highway 36 northwest of
Red Bluff. Leaving Paskenta,
take Corrigan and Lowery Roads.
Be sure to turn north on Hesse,
west on Johnson, and north
again on Masten. Drive slowly
for it is open-range cattle country.
Turn west on Reeds Creek Road
to Vestal Road and through open
gates, past old barns, hills,
mountains, wildflowers, fording
streams from time to time.
You'll make it!
There are several ways to reach
Redding from here. It is
your choice.

COYOTE,
BEYOND NEWVILLE

The Bell Springs Road into Trinity National Forest

Bell Springs is a gravel road beginning
12 miles north of Laytonville off Highway 101.

There were deer and ground squirrels
and views of mountain ranges on
both sides of this ridge road.
The unusual "Island Mountain"
is viewed many times and
from differing aspects as
you proceed along this
back road. At Harris you
have an opportunity
to return to Highway 101
at Garberville, or continue,
as I did, northeast to
Alderpoint and Zenia.

ISLAND MOUNTAIN,
BELL SPRINGS ROAD

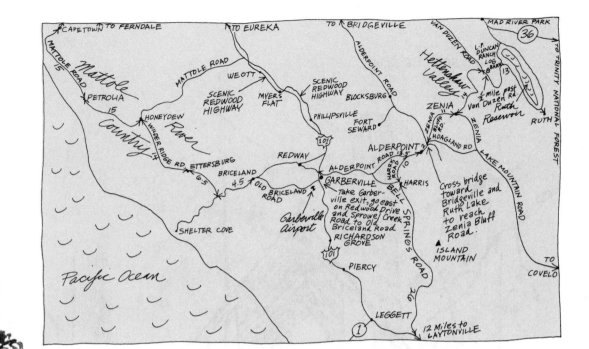

The population of Zenia was 2 people, 2 dogs, and one cat at the time of my visit. The owner of the old store informed me that the town was named by a little girl, long ago, whose favorite flower was a "Zenia" (or, Zinnia, if you'd rather).

ZENIA STORE, CIRCA 1910

LOG BARN, HETTENSHAW VALLEY

Zenia Bluff Road continues through Six Rivers
National Forest. Hettenshaw valley got
its name from a native plant that Indians
gathered in earlier times for food. They
called it "KETTEN-CHOW," I was told by an
Indian resident at Duncan Ranch.
Zenia Road eventually reaches Ruth
Reservoir and Lower Mad River Road
to Highway 36 and on to Trinity
National Forest.

Mattole River Country

Go west from Garberville and Highway 101 on the old Briceland Road, then 4½ miles farther, to turn north on Ettersburg-Honeydew Road. This is Mattole River Country.

The land is mountainous and covered with forests of young fir, red-berried madrone, and thick stands of tan-bark oak.

HONEYDEW STORE AND POST OFFICE

The town of Ettersburg has disappeared, but Honeydew Store is still open, and so is the post office. According to the postmaster, in the old days there was a grove of cottonwood trees down by the river. Early settlers found dew each morning on tarpaulins spread beneath the cottonwoods. The dew tasted sweet to them, so the place was named "Honeydew."
You drive past Petrolia to the ocean, then inland over the hills to the town of Ferndale. Grizzly Bluff Road from Ferndale takes you past the many-gabled Grizzly Bluff School and on to Highway 101.

GUMDROP TREES, ARNOLD BERDING HOUSE, FERNDALE, 1875

Trinity Alps Loop

French Gulch is 3 miles north of Highway 299 on Trinity Mountain Road, some 15 miles west of Redding. This begins the loop.

Trinity Mountain Road winds up into Shasta National Forest, and at the top you can see all of the Trinity Alps in blue and purple splendor. Farther on, Mt. Shasta and row upon row of mountain ridges come into view.

CHURCH AT FRENCH GULCH,
TRINITY MOUNTAIN ROAD

Joss House, 1874,
Weaverville

After completing the loop around
Lake Engle you can return to 299 at
Weaverville to see the 1874 Chinese
Joss House. I sketched the edifice
from the shade of a locust tree, deep
lawn under my feet, my shoes off.

Klamath National Forest
and the Marble Mountains Loop

Highway 299 above Arcata on Highway 101
goes east 6 miles to Blue Lake and Korbel.
From here north is a trip through dense
forests and mountains.

At Willow Creek Highway 96 goes to
Somes Bar, Happy Camp, and Hamburg.
From here you can go south to
Etna, Sawyer's Bar, Forks of the
Salmon, eventually returning
to Arcata and Eureka.

LOG PILE AT KORBEL

At Forks of the Salmon a tiny graveyard lines one side of the narrow road. There was a fiddler's grave in it appropriately decorated by a fiddle as headstone. At the post office I asked about the grave and was told that it was Frank Rimmer's, "who made some mighty fine music in his time." The postmaster's brother-in-law made the violin to place on Rimmer's grave in memory of this contribution to humankind. I asked a local inhabitant how to correctly spell Rimmer's last name, then spelled it as best I could. He said, "That's close enough."

EPILOGUE

On the back roads of California I rediscovered the pleasure of driving. It had nothing to do with haste, and everything to do with taking time to perceive, with full consciousness, the earth's ever-changing colors, designs, and patterns. The most satisfying roads and byways followed the contour of the land, and that is why I deplore the gouging and cleaving of the earth's surface, the straightening of roads for the sake of speed. My hope is that the best of the back roads will be maintained, but not "improved." We must pick up a share of the litter left by despoilers, support efforts toward vehicles that do not pollute the air, and back measures that will return quality, beauty, and naturalness to the land. I believe we must look to the needs of our planet earth over and above the immediate needs of mankind.

A bamboo pen ⬤▭, fashioned by me, was used for most of the "Back Roads" drawings. Black, waterproof ink was my medium, along with a bottle of diluted ink for grey tones. A Rapidograph ▭▭▭ pen was used for the line drawings and lettering, and 70 lb. watercolor paper was the sketching material.

Good traveling!

EARL THOLLANDER